SO-BZX-999

31 DAYS OF PRAYER

The Father's Heart
Recovery for The Nation

LINDA HANRATTY

31 DAYS OF PRAYER

By Linda Hanratty

www.31dop.org
© 2020 Tillamook Countywide Prayer Team.
All rights reserved.

This book or parts thereof may not be reproduced in any form, stored in retrieval systems, or transmitted in any form by any means-electronic, mechanical, photocopy, recording, or otherwise-without prior written permission of the publisher, except as provided by United States copyright law.

Scripture taken from the New King James Version®. Copyright © 1982 by Thomas Nelson. Used by permission. All rights reserved.

Acknowledgements

Our profound thanks to the inspired contributors who made this book a reality. Cullis James Autry, Sandy Blaser, Terry Blaser, Gary Christerson, Julie Christerson, Pastor Jeff Coon, Pastor Dean Crist, Jim Donohue, Lydia Donohue, Mike Hanratty, Linda Hanratty, Lacey Hawkins, Pastor Marv Kasemeier, Pastor Erin McMahan, Pastor Justin McMahan, Pam Neighbor, Lauri Norman, Eric Swanson, Suzanne Weber and others who wish to remain anonymous.

Edited by Linda Hanratty and Terry Blaser

Cover Design by Ray Hopfer

Published by   50 Days of Prayer
1000 Main Street, Suite 12
Tillamook, OR 97141
www.50dop.org

e-book   ISBN 978-1-952515-07-1
paperback   ISBN 978-1-952515-06-4

1.1

www.31dop.org - For current information about this book
www.50dop.org - For other resources published by Tillamook Countywide Prayer Team

TABLE OF CONTENTS

Appendices:

Forward

I believe this prayer book is for NOW: 'such a time as this'. As we live in today's political, economic and social climates and head into the fall elections, our nation needs our prayers more than any other thing.

"**What can I do** about what's going on?" you may ask?

1. The MOST effective thing you can do is to **PRAY** in faith.
2. Next, you can **ENCOURAGE** others to seek God in prayer asking Him to intervene in our country.
3. Finally, you can **VOTE** for candidates who uphold godly values.

This is a season which calls for ALL Christians to rise up and take a stand against the forces of darkness that so boldly attempt to threaten us.

In the pages that follow are **31 prayers for 31 days**. Hopefully, God's people will begin this prayer guide August 1st and repeat it in September and October. I urge you to tell others about it so that more and more people will be actively praying for this homeland we love: One Nation Under God!

Eze 22:30-31 "So I sought for a man among them who would make a wall, and stand in the gap before Me on behalf of the land, that I should not destroy it; but I found no one. "Therefore, I have poured out My indignation on them; I have consumed them with the fire of My wrath; and I have recompensed their deeds on their own heads," says the Lord God.

'Lord, I believe there are thousands of intercessors crying out for our nation to be forgiven, righted and restored! Thank You for hearing, moving, and healing our land.'

Since the beginning of 2020, our nation and the world have witnessed rapid change and trauma: school, business and church shut-downs across the nation due to COVID-19, a crashing economy, record breaking unemployment, shortages, etc. We have been required to learn and practice social distancing. We have witnessed anarchy, revelry and crime committed by individuals who have attempted to take over cities and neighborhoods and erase our history by tearing down monuments. Some of what we have treasured as 'good' is now being labeled as 'evil'. Conversely, what was known as 'evil', is now being applauded as 'good', 'open-minded', or 'tolerance'. Cities and lawmakers have moved to defund instead of to defend our police and law enforcements, thereby removing lawful protocols and their ability to protect and serve. The Christian values and constitutional rights which have set this nation apart from all others are being eroded.

<u>We must not stand by idly and watch!</u> Press in and engage in the battle by praying! God has given us the authority as sons and daughters of Jesus Christ to stand in the gap to pray His word and will. We can minister confession, repentance, and cry out for forgiveness as in the city of Nineveh in the Book of Jonah. We can cry to God for His mercy and forgive those who intend to restrict our freedoms. Our most powerful weapon is to LOVE our enemies, those who spitefully use us. We can do this in prayer.

This book is a compilation of powerful prayers for today. They are written by pastors and intercessors from many different churches. You will notice the writer's different personalities reflected, and the strength and inspiration of the Holy Spirit in the words expressed. These prayers are gifts from intercessors who have pressed in to hear the Lord's heart. On behalf of the writers, I submit these prayers to you and to our Lord.

"Let us therefore come boldly to the throne of grace, that we may obtain mercy and find grace to help in time of need." Heb. 4:16

Remember that God is on His throne: Ps. 103:19. He is our refuge and our strength: Ps. 46. He is God, Omnipotent: "I have made the earth, and created man on it. I—My hands—stretched out the heavens, and all their host I have commanded." Is. 45:12 "... And there is no other God besides Me, a just God and a Savior; there is none besides Me. Look to Me, and be saved, all you ends of the earth! For I am God, and there is no other." Is. 45:21-22.

This is a season of sorrows for our nation and for the world. Jesus talked about this in Matt. 24:4-8 and Mark 13:5-8. It implores "face-time" (on our face) with the Father. We invite you to pray these prayers out loud; include your family, friends and prayer partners. Cry out to the Lord and let these prayers catapult your prayer life to a new realm.

May He, the God of all comfort grant you peace and protection and draw you ever closer to His heart. – LH

Day 1

Call to Arm for Battle

Isaiah 6:8-10 I heard the voice of the Lord, saying: "Whom shall I send, and who will go for Us?" Then I said, "Here am I, Send me."

Ezekiel 22:30 So I sought for a man among them who would make a wall, and stand in the gap before Me on behalf of the land, that I should not destroy it; but I found no one.

An Exhortation:

My Child...I'm searching the world to and fro for those who love me, who know the power of Prayer and will eagerly take a stand. I ask you...Will you stand in the gap for your city...for your state and nation? 'Do not be afraid or discouraged because of this vast army. For the battle is not yours, but God's. You will not need to fight in this battle. Position yourselves, stand still and see the salvation of the Lord, who is with you, ... Do not fear or be dismayed; ...go out against them, for the Lord is with you (2 Chronicles 20:15-17) Therefore, as you are faithful to pray and seek the face of God...The Lord will march out like a champion, like a warrior He will stir up his zeal; with a shout He will raise the battle cry and will triumph over his enemies. (Isaiah 42:13) Who is this King of glory? The Lord strong and mighty, the Lord mighty in battle!! (Psalm 24:8) Therefore, it is an upmost importance to ready yourself to war by putting on...The Armor of God. So, arm yourselves before the Lord for the war. (Numbers 32:20) Put on the whole armor of God, that you may be able to stand against the wiles of the devil. (Ephesians 6:11)

Prayer:

Oh Lord, as we meditate upon these scriptures, and prayers penned upon these pages, may the words sink deeply into the soil of our hearts, bringing forth a harvest of righteousness - all for the glory and honor of Your Holy Name..... We thank You for all Your promises, so we boldly enter the land without fear...for the battle belongs to You Lord!! Help us enter Your Courts with praise, thanksgiving, faith and boldness, for the weapons of warfare are not carnal but mighty in God for pulling down strongholds. (2 Corinthians 10:4)

Personal prayer:

Lord, help me to be strong in the Lord and in His mighty power. I clothe myself in heavenly armor... putting on the full armor of God, so that I may take my stand against the devil's schemes. For my struggle is not against flesh and blood, but against the rulers, against the authorities, against the powers of this dark world and against the spiritual forces of evil in the heavenly realms. Therefore, I put on the full armor of God, so that when the day of evil comes, I may be able to stand my ground, and after I have done everything, to stand. Lord, help me stand firm, with the belt of truth buckled around my waist, with the breastplate of righteousness in place and with my feet fitted with the readiness that comes from the gospel of peace. In addition to all this, I take up the shield of faith, with which I can extinguish all the flaming arrows of the evil one. I take up the helmet of salvation and the sword of the Spirit, which is the powerful Word of God. Having done all, help me stand! (Ephesians 6:13)

Oh, Lord, as I stand clothed in Your righteousness, armed for battle, help me be alert and always looking to You, the author and finisher of my faith! Give me ears to hear Your voice and a heart sensitive to Your Holy Spirit. I ask for wisdom to know how to pray powerfully with understanding using Your Word to pray, because it is mighty, and it does not return void without accomplishing what You sent it for. Yes, Lord…I accept your invitation to join my brothers and sisters in Christ. Together, let us form a battle line of prayer that will shake this nation. Together, may we boldly stand our ground and see the goodness of the Lord in the land of living! (Psalm 27:13) (1 Sam 12:16)

For whatever is born of God overcomes the world. And this is the victory that has overcome the world—our faith. Who is he who overcomes the world, but he who believes that Jesus is the Son of God? 1 John 5:4-5

I thank you Heavenly Father for giving us your Son Jesus Christ and for His sacrificial work on the cross. Thank You that He has already overcome the world. I place all my faith in Christ alone. It is through Christ, I too am a victorious overcomer, born of the Spirit and clothed in His righteousness! Lord, I hear your call…. I realize our nation is in a "Spiritual Battle". Therefore, help me commit to daily devoting time in prayer and seeking Your face. Help me live each passing day guided by your Spirit and Truth, bringing glory and honor to Your holy name. Together with Christ I will be a victorious warrior!! – In Jesus Name, Amen.

Day 2

Recovery from the Coronavirus

Scripture:
Matthew 5: 4,6,7,9

⁴Blessed are those who mourn,
For they shall be comforted.
⁶Blessed are those who hunger and thirst for righteousness,
For they shall be filled.
⁷Blessed are the merciful,
For they shall obtain mercy.
⁹Blessed are the peacemakers,
For they shall be called sons of God.

Psalm 91

Abba Father, we come before Your throne of grace to find help for a hurting world. A world smitten by a plague that has brought death and destruction to nearly every nation. Lord, we cry out for mercy and help. We are a weak and sinful people. As a world-wide culture we have sinned against You and man. We come before You crying out for forgiveness. We come before You with repentant hearts. We ask that You break the yoke of infirmity that has covered our nation and world. We cry out for healing in every sector. Turn the heart of our nation toward You during this season.

We ask for healing to those who have been sick with coronavirus. We ask for Christians to rise up, care for the sick, and minister hope to the hurting. We bind the spirit of fear in Jesus' name, and cry out for more faith. We ask for strength and wisdom for our healthcare workers and an extra measure of protection from the virus. We lift up areas which have been overwhelmed by the virus.

Lord, we ask that You inactivate the virulence of this virus and turn it into a spoiled and defeated foe. Strengthen our God-built immune systems to resist disease and be overcomers. We ask for special grace over our elders. We pray for scientists and doctors to find amazing new treatments and strategies to meet needs and speed recoveries. We ask for herd immunity in our general population and that vaccines will not be required.

We cry out to the Passover Lamb, to paint the doorposts of our homes, cities, state and nation with the Blood of Jesus, for the protection we seek. We cry out for strength. Let every heart be sensitive to Your Holy Spirit. Expose darkness and eradicate political schemes that have used this wounded season to pursue ungodly purposes. Lord, undo what the enemy has meant for evil. We cry out for safe re-openings of our churches, schools, businesses, and government and that this affliction would not rise up again. We ask for godly wisdom for each step of re-opening. We ask that instead of a second or third wave of the coronavirus, there would be wave after wave of Your healing presence and glory released across the face of the earth!

We ask that You cause Your redemption to flow through this nation like a river, touching everything in its wake. Let it be on earth as it is in heaven. In Jesus Name, Amen

Day 3

Rebuilding the Church after COVID-19 Assimilation

James 1:5 *If any of you lacks wisdom, let him ask of God, who gives to all liberally and without reproach, and it will be given to him.*

Philippians 2:3-4 *"Let nothing be done through selfish ambition or conceit, but in lowliness of mind let each esteem others better than himself. Let each of you look out not only for his own interests, but also for the interest of others."*

Father, thank you for the church, the body of Christ. Thank you for the giftings and abilities You have placed within each of us to edify and build up one another for Your glory.

Jesus, You said You would not leave us as orphans when You went to the Father. You gave us Your Holy Spirit, our "Helper" who would be with us forever (Jn 14:16, 18). What an incomprehensible and re-assuring truth to ponder and live!! Father, we ask for Holy Spirit-inspired wisdom to equip us as we, Your church, co-labor according to Your will. In the past several months, we've learned to do church a whole different way. You've given us wisdom to accomplish that through many new means. Thank You, Lord. Now give us wisdom as we reconnect.

Thank You that many thousands of people have tuned in for the first time and made commitments to follow You during online church ser-vices. Now, we ask that You cause them to hunger and thirst for right-eousness. Help them get established in a local bible-preaching church and body of Christ. Help them put down deep roots in Your Word

(Matt 13:1-8). Help them grow like healthy plants in good soil into the fullness of Your calling for them.

Father, it is Your desire that we connect with one another to encourage, love, strengthen and to bless the Body of Christ. Take away all fear from our hearts that would in any way keep us from reconnecting in our churches. We need one another. You have told us that perfect love casts out fear (1 Jn 4:18). Give me so much love for my brothers and sisters in Christ that fear would not be present when we join together in prayer and worship (Col. 3:15). Holy Spirit speak to every heart. Use this season to develop depth and Your purpose in the Body of Christ. Cause Your church to shine as a beacon of light for all to see. Draw the lost to Your light. Assimilate them into the body.

As we come together, let us do as the apostle Paul instructs us and be unwavering in our love and devotion to one another. (Rom. 12:10-13) Help us understand and pray for one another. Help us show the world what it means to live for the Lord. It's so easy to get caught up in the political factions taking place. It's so easy to take sides regarding the news of the day. The enemy would love to divide us. But, not on my watch! I will not be a tool of the enemy, but a vessel for Father's use.

Father, forgive me for not loving my church family as I ought. Forgive me for allowing fear to rule my heart rather than the peace of God. Forgive me for allowing my own personal interests to be more important than the needs of my spiritual family. Work out of me "self", so that You can use me for the benefit of others; so that You will be exalted. People need Jesus. Help me to not miss any opportunity to minister Christ to others. In Jesus' holy name I pray. Amen

Day 4

The Modern-Day Leader
Facing a Complex World

Scripture: Psalm 18:18-30, Ephesians 4:12-16

Protection: Lord, we lift up our church pastors and leaders of today. When Your people step up into ministry, it is like a giant bull's-eye is placed on their backs and the enemy would like nothing more than to destroy them before they step into the purpose You have put before them. We pray for Your supernatural protection around them and their families, physically, mentally, spiritually, financially, in everything they do and everywhere they go.

Support: We pray that You surround them with people who will encourage and support them to remember what Your word says in Isaiah 41:10: 'that You are with them, You will strengthen them, You will help them and You will uphold them with Your righteous right hand.' We also pray that You surround them with leaders who will speak into their lives and help them to be accountable: not falling into the traps of the enemy; but "guarding their hearts" as Proverbs 4:23 says, "for everything they do flows from it."

Wisdom for leadership: We pray that Your leaders would have Your wisdom in how they lead. The first person they have to lead properly is themselves, so we pray that every leader would submit themselves first to Your leadership, God, and Your wisdom on how to lead. Then, as they lead others, we pray that they would do so from a place of humility, honesty and love of God. We, as leaders, ask for Your forgiveness in the areas of pride, dishonesty and when we did not walk in love. We pray that if we or other leaders have allowed these things to come between You and our leadership that Your sovereign hand would convict us and challenge us to turn from our sins and come into submission under You. We pray that as every leader is forgiven and cleansed that they would be refreshed and protected from falling into the trap of becoming as Galatians 6:9 says "weary in well doing" and, thus, not fulfilling Your purpose for their lives.

Leading like Jesus did: We pray that all leaders would have a renewed focus of leading in the method like Jesus did. In John 13:13-17 He says, "I have set for you an example that you should do as I have." Regarding loving people and having compassion for those outside the church in a complex and constantly changing world, we pray that each leader would look to Jesus' example with those outside of His circle. When considering the challenges that are before our leaders, we pray they would apply Jesus' messages of love as in His parable of the Good Samaritan, and also in how He interacted with the Samaritan woman at the well. We pray that His life of love is what we would seek to emulate.

Humility: In all of this we pray that our leaders would lead us with sacrificial humility as Jesus did. Just as Jesus washed the feet of His disciples in John 10:42-45 we pray that our leaders take His attitude of servant leadership.

Vision to prepare the people for the ministry: We pray that they would look intently at Your Son's example with the disciples. Give our leaders Your ideas on how to raise and prepare people for the ministry work that is set before each of them; burn Your vision and passion for the world, into our hearts. The harvest fields are white. We cry out to You, the Lord of the harvest to raise up laborers. Lord, remove the hindrances and fears that have limited believers and the church's vision for the people on the other side of our walls. Birth in each of us a love for them. Help us reach them. Give the Church a vision to bring in the harvest and give the world a vision to come in seeking You. Bring that wall down. Release Your love into our communities. Help us raise up new and motivated leaders who have vision according to Your will. Let the Body of Christ - each member - develop a vision of sharing Your love. Equip them to give an answer of the hope that lives within them. Help them lead people to Your throne of grace. Let them be equipped with an Ephesians 4:11 mentality of "Team Ministry". Let each one grow to their full potential calling in You, serving You, serving one another in love, and serving our community. Let us be authors and finishers in the faith, persevering with endurance and patience.

Lord, we thank You for our leaders and we pray for Your blessings in their lives. We pray that as they navigate one of the most complex leadership roles they will ever step into, that You will be their provider in every area. Bless them in all their ways as they sacrifice, set an example, live out a life of compassion and do it while consistently laying their lives down before You in humility. In Jesus Name, Amen

Day 5

Discipleship/Multiplication

Romans 10:14-15 *"How then shall they call on Him in whom they have not believed? And how shall they believe in Him of whom they have not heard? And how shall they hear without a preacher? And how shall they preach unless they are sent? As it is written: 'How beautiful are the feet of those who preach the gospel of peace, who bring glad tidings of good things.'"*

Acts 1:8 *"But you shall receive power when the Holy Spirit has come upon you; and you shall be witnesses to Me in Jerusalem and in all Judea and Samaria, and to the end of the earth."*

II Timothy 2:2 *"And the things that you have heard from me among many witnesses, commit these to faithful men who will be able to teach others also."*

Dear Lord, we thank You that during and in the aftermath of this great spiritual awakening taking place, your people will not be content to only revel in their new freedom, but will be compelled by Your Spirit to bring the good news to others who will then, in turn, bring it to others.

We bind up the spirit of selfishness and false contentment that would cause us to stay comfortably where we are, and ask that You would give us Your eyes to see the brokenness in the world around us and Your heart of compassion to show it Your healing. We know that we cannot do this effectively in our own strength or wisdom, so we humbly, but expectantly rely on the Holy Spirit to empower us to reach our communities. Because You said that You would send workers for the harvest when we pray, we ask that You would highlight to us people of peace into which You would have us pour Your word into. Father, we know that Your heart is to reach all people unto the ends of the earth. So right now, at this time in history, we believe and contend for disciples to be birthed for several generations of disciple-making.

Today, we lay down our foolish pride, false ambitions and personal ambitions on the altar of unity. You have said that the hurting world will know us by our love for one another (John 17), so we purpose to extend grace to each other, repent when we do wrong and forgive when wrong is done to us so we may accomplish Your great commission together.
In Jesus' mighty name, Amen.

Day 6

Casting our Nets and Working Together in Unity

Matthew 13:47 Again, the kingdom of heaven is like a dragnet that was cast into the sea and gathered some of every kind, (fish)

John 21:6 "And He said to <u>them</u>, "Cast the net on the right side of the boat, and you will find some." So they cast, and now they were not able to draw it in because of the multitude of fish."

Revelation 7:9-10 After these things I looked, and behold, a great multitude which no one could number, of all nations, tribes, peoples, and tongues, standing before the throne and before the Lamb ... 10 and crying out with a loud voice, saying, "Salvation belongs to our God who sits on the throne, and to the Lamb!"

1 Cor. 12:13-16 For by one Spirit we were all baptized into one body— whether Jews or Greeks, whether slaves or free—and have all been made to drink into one Spirit. 14 For in fact the body is not one member but many.

John 17:20-21 "I do not pray for these alone, but also for those who will believe in Me through their word; 21 that they all may be one, as You, Father, are in Me, and I in You; that they also may be one in Us, that the world may believe that You sent Me.

John 14:27 Peace I leave with you, My peace I give to you; not as the world gives do I give to you. Let not your heart be troubled, neither let it be afraid.

Father, You have called all kinds of people -- every nation, tribe, people and language -- to be the Body of Christ. We cannot effectively function apart from one another (I Cor 12). We are one body, one church, with many parts, working together to make a whole body. Lord, You, made us into one body by uniting us in You. This is an exceedingly great gift and we are grateful. Forgive us for failing to recognize the value in each part of Your body. If the kingdom of Heaven is like a net, and we the Church are together holding the net, then we are stronger to bring in an exceedingly great harvest of many kinds of people. We ask that You strengthen the churches to create a very strong relational net to bring in and retain a very large harvest. We know and desire to work together to accomplish this great task!

Father, we ask You to give Your church peace and even rejoicing in the differences between our churches. Jesus, You left us with Your peace when You returned to the Father. Let your church remain in Your peace and work together. Help our pastors and leadership walk in faith not fear! Help us walk in true friendship with one another, and unity in You. Keep us from falling into the enemy's trap of fear and isolation from our brothers and sisters in Christ. Father, You have also given Your church the Holy Spirit, who is with us. Thank You for Your presence! As a church we choose to believe and act on your words. Help us know Your word and handle it accurately. Though bad news is all around us may Your words dwell within us. We declare You are our firm foundation.

Father unite Your church around the Lord Jesus Christ. Unite us in Your love. Not a love that originates from us but Your love. Give us a love that pushes through our different giftings. Help us to recognize and appreciate the various parts of the Body of Christ. Bring us together as the complete Body of Christ working together in love under Jesus' headship.

Father strengthen us to remain on mission! We know nothing surprises you and that every trial presents opportunities for your church to 'be the Church'. Help us to see, hear and understand what you are saying to Your church, then obey and reach out in service to our nation and the world. Jesus, help us see like You see, and recognize everyone's great value regardless of the color of their skin. Give us Your boldness to witness in truth and deeds, modeling unity so others will come to know Jesus as Savior.

Father, unite us in mission. We believe there is a great harvest that is ready now to be harvested. Lord of the Harvest "send out" workers all over the world. In Revelation, You show us a heavenly event of worship. The worshippers are from EVERY nation, tribe, people, and language. Lord of the Harvest, unite Your church so this mighty harvest will be brought in to Your kingdom. In Jesus name we ask Amen!

Day 7

Raise Up Intercessors, Here I Am Send Me

SCRIPTURE:

Ezekiel 22:30 *So I sought for a man among them who would make a wall, and stand in the gap before Me on behalf of the land, that I should not destroy it; but I found no one.*

Job 22: 21-23,27,28,30 *" ²¹Now acquaint yourself with Him, and be at peace; Thereby good will come to you. ²² Receive, please, instruction from His mouth, And lay up His words in your heart. For then you will have your delight in the Almighty, ²³ If you return to the Almighty, you will be built up; You will remove iniquity far from your tents. And lift up your face to God. ²⁷ You will make your prayer to Him, He will hear you, And you will pay your vows. ²⁸ You will also declare a thing, And it will be established for you; So light will shine on your ways. ³⁰ He will even deliver one who is not innocent; Yes, he will be delivered by the purity of your hands."*

James 5:16 *The effective, fervent prayer of a righteous man avails much.*

PRAYER:

Holy and Righteous God. You have called us, Your children, those who call You, Lord, to intercede on behalf of our people, churches, cities, state, nation and world. You have called the whole Body of Christ to rise up and declare Your Name, the name above every other name, to glorify You and to bow before You. Holy Spirit, we come humbly, asking to hear Your heart. Give us ears to hear Your voice, eyes to see and a heart that loves like You love. As we stand in faith

19

praying to You, we declare this to be Holy Ground. Your Word promises that if there was one intercessor to build a wall and stand in the gap before You on behalf of the land (our churches, city, state and nation), that You should not destroy it... Lord, we are MANY intercessors! So, we rejoice and cry out to raise up the intercessors in every church, in every city, state and nation! We thank You that You have blessed us with this promise, and we take You at Your Word. You have given us Your Word to do battle. We thank You for the call to declare and decree a thing (Your Word) and it will be established! So, we declare that You are our God! All praise and glory goes to You, the King Eternal, the Ruler over all, our Messiah. Let Your scepter be extended to us, Your children as we petition You, to save us from our sin, and the iniquity that has fallen on us as a nation, and to cry out for restoration. Rebuild our walls. Thank you for washing us with the water of Your Word and cleansing us from our sin with Your precious blood. Let it be on earth as it is in Heaven! We call it forth! Let the Church of Jesus Christ arise in power and glory!

And Jesus, my King. You are merciful and kind. Forgive me when I have not engaged in prayer but instead complained. When I do not watch my words, I so easily sin and disable my faith. Let faith arise in ME! Let the Word of the Lord arise in ME! Let righteous and holy boldness arise in ME. Awake me from my slumber! You have called ME to report for duty and I say, "Here I am, send me!" And I mean it! Help me to make faith filled, mighty earth shaking, nation healing prayers part of my daily walk. I am Yours and You are mine! I do not do this in my own strength, but in Your Holy and Mighty Name! The Joy of the Lord is my strength. You have clothed me with a garment of praise. You equip me for every good thing! Let me not shrink back from the calling. In Jesus Mighty Name, Amen!

Day 8

Protection from Evil

Romans 8:37-39 ... we are more than conquerors through Him who loved us. For I am persuaded that neither death nor life, nor angels nor principalities nor powers, nor things present nor things to come, nor height nor depth, nor any other created thing, shall be able to separate us from the love of God which is in Christ Jesus our Lord.

2 Timothy 1:7; Psalm 91:1-16; Psalm 27:1

PRAYER:

O Lord, as we walk in the midst of troubled times, shield, protect and strengthen the Body of Christ throughout the world from the evil one. Let our faith arise even in the midst of all the turmoil! For You have not given us a spirit of fear, but of power and of love and of a sound mind....You, promise to never leave us nor forsake us. Therefore, when darkness surrounds us, let us boldly confess "The Lord is My Helper; whom shall I fear?" Lord we look to You...A Strong Tower of Refuge, Our Rock; Our Shield, and the Horn of our Salvation, Our Savior...Our Deliverer...You are the Resurrection of Life! You are our Hiding Place; You preserve us from trouble; and surround us with songs of deliverance. Remind us Lord that we as humans are no match for the enemy...our help must come from the Lord! Therefore, when darkness surrounds us, let us be quick to call upon the name of the Lord...Our Defender...Our protection...Our Faithful God, in whom we trust!

May the Body of Christ hear Your call to prepare for battle...To arise to their rightful place with a dynamic holy boldness! May we stand firm on the Holy Word as we face adversity and not fear the terror of night, nor the arrow that flies by day, nor the pestilence that stalks in the darkness, nor the plague that destroys at midday...!! O God empower your people to be strong in the Lord, and fully trust Your Holy Word...For you have provided the weapons to demolish strongholds through Your word and the spirit-empowered prayer! Remind us to daily put on the whole armor of God, that we may be able to stand against the devil's schemes...for we know we wrestle not against flesh and blood,....Therefore, prompt us to put on the full armor of God, so that when the day of evil comes, we may be able to stand our ground, praying for one another!

Thank you for your mighty protection, Lord...For who shall separate us from the love of Christ? Shall trouble or hardship or persecution or famine or nakedness or danger or sword? As it is written, "...We are more than conquerors through Him who loved us...nothing will be able to separate us from the love of God that is in Christ Jesus our Lord."

Lord may our Brothers and Sisters in Christ seek you with all their hearts and be filled to overflowing with the Light of Your Presence!! Help us NOT be afraid to love and encourage others, even in the midst of dark times.

Bless the Lord O my soul.... For You never sleep nor slumber… You are constantly watching and caring for Your people! — Keeping us from all harm— You will forever keep guard over our lives...our coming and going, both now and forevermore. With God as our Defender.... who can be against us?

*And now, Lord, I submit areas of my life to You that cause me fear and anxiety, and I repent for entertaining them. I confess them as faithlessness. They are _____. You have given me Your

Word to overcome ALL the power of the evil one, even in my own mind. Today, I lay my fears at Your throne of grace. Help me to walk free from these and leave them with You. Fill me with Your Holy Spirit and Faith to walk boldly and in victory over ALL these things. In Jesus Name! Amen!

Day 9

Healing of Hearts for Those Who Have Lost Loved Ones

*For I will turn their mourning to joy, Will comfort them, And make them rejoice rather than sorrow (**Jeremiah 31:13**)*

*Jesus said to her, "I am the resurrection and the life. He who believes in Me, though he may die, he shall live. And whoever lives and believes in Me shall never die." (**John 11:25-26**)*

*My flesh and my heart may fail, but God is the strength of my heart and my portion forever. (**Psalm 73:26**)*

Heavenly Father, I come to You with a heavy heart. So many precious lives have been lost due to the COVID-19 pandemic. Many families are now faced with grief and cannot imagine how to survive this dark hour. Father, may You surround those families with Your love. And for those who may be facing this alone, I ask You, Lord, to send someone to care, to wipe the tears and to have a listening ear.

The death of a loved one is an unthinkable loss that no one is ever prepared to face. Lord, please embrace each one mourning in Your loving arms. May Your touch bring healing and restoration to the broken, grieving hearts. Give peace to their wounded souls and bless them with the strength to face each new day. Lord, I pray for Your healing waters to flow freely over those in despair bringing comfort, rest and peace.

I pray those who are hurting will call upon You and look to You as Savior, healer, comforter and friend. May their faith in Christ remain steadfast. Help each hurting heart to look beyond the grave to the living hope of eternity. As their eyes are fixed upon Jesus, may their mourning be turned into joy while celebrating the life of their loved one! With Your strength may they find a way to continue to live, love and even laugh again.

Oh Lord, the pain of grief can be so devastating and there simply isn't an answer to the question "why?" But Thank You Lord. With Your help, beyond all the tears and the heartache, somehow the clouds of grief do have a way of lessening with time; for You are "the resurrection and the life!"

Now, Lord, I ask that You help me to be sensitive to those who have lost family members during this season. Let me be an instrument of Your peace. Where there is darkness, let me sow light, where there is pain & suffering, let me sow comfort, help me to practice the art of "presence even without words" to bring Your love flooding in. I lift up:_____. I ask a special blessing on their lives, now. Strengthen them to fight the good fight of faith, looking to You, the God of all comfort. Help me be a person who goes toward those who are hurting rather than turning my face. Give me courage, Lord. I want to be a conduit of Your love.
In Jesus' name, Amen

Day 10

Healthcare Recovery

1 Peter 5:7   *Casting all your care upon Him, for He cares for you.*

Galatians 6:9   *And let us not grow weary while doing good, for in due season we shall reap if we do not lose heart.*

1 Corinthians 12:4-7 *⁴There are diversities of gifts, but the same Spirit. ⁵There are differences of ministries, but the same Lord. ⁶And there are diversities of activities, but it is the same God who works all in all. ⁷But the manifestation of the Spirit is given to each one for the profit of all:*

Philippians 4:6   *Be anxious for nothing, but in everything by prayer and supplication, with thanksgiving, let your requests be made known to God;*

PRAYER:

Restoration: Lord, our hospitals, clinics and all forms of health care have been put on hold to protect our people during the COVID-19 pandemic. We thank You for your protection over the people we serve of this land during this season. We ask now, as the health care industry resumes full operations that You guide, grant wisdom and protection to every facility, every administrator, every health care worker. Release the gifts of Your Holy Spirit to be actively working in our health care systems bringing hope, peace and strength. We ask that You restore financial resources and a full re-engagement of the facilities. For systems that were faulty or put on hold, or systems that were emancipated during this period of shut-down, use this wisdom to re-shape how we do things. Help the health care industry glean what was good and overcome challenges. We pray for an improved health care system as a result of this pandemic. Guide our health care leaders with Your eye and show them the way.

Health Care Workers: Loving God, You created us with the capacity to be your hands and feet as we provide healing to Your children. Thank You for the diversity of gifts You have given our health care workers to meet needs. Give us strength, courage and discernment to do Your work in these uncertain times. We are fighting an enemy that we have never had to fight before. We humbly ask that You pour out an extra measure of Your blessing and protection on our health care workers. We know that You care for them.

Wholeness: As we fight COVID-19 we ask that we see Your healing touch in those that are fighting this battle. Please restore them to health and do not let them grow weary; give them the courage to press on, even in the darkest hour.

Hope: Lord God, in every interaction, in every encounter, please let us give the one thing that we most desire – hope. Hope for a future without disease, hope for a world without strife, and hope for eternal life with You.

We pray for all the physicians, nurses, and health care providers; may they be blessed with the wisdom and grace needed to provide the best care possible and honor You in all that they do.

In Jesus Name, Amen.

Day 11

Recovery of The Economy and Businesses

Luke 12:15 *And He said to them, "Take heed and beware of covet-ousness, for one's life does not consist in the abundance of the things he possesses."*

Phil 4:19 *And my God shall supply all your need according to His riches in glory by Christ Jesus.*

2 Chron 7:13-14 *"When I shut up heaven and there is no rain, or command the locusts to devour the land, or send pestilence among My people, "if My people who are called by My name will humble them-selves, and pray and seek My face, and turn from their wicked ways, then I will hear from heaven, and will forgive their sin and heal their land.*

Dear Father, We ask for Your forgiveness in the name and shed blood of Jesus. Forgive us for our greed and selfish ways and not honoring You in all our ways. Forgive us when we look to ourselves and rely on our skills, proficiencies and abilities to provide things and we forget that everything we have comes from You.

Father, we pray for our economy. We pray for a strong and vibrant economy based on reality and not speculation. In recent months, it has ridden a roller coaster of highs and lows. It has faltered under the COVID-19 pandemic, the stock market, civil unrest, and world-wide uncertainties of failed economies, wars, famines, disease, and strife.

We pray for the small businesses and their employees who have been the backbone of America. We pray for the large industries. We pray for the millions of workers who have lost their jobs, who have been furloughed or who are on unemployment. Many can't make monthly payments and face losing homes, cars, etc. Many have been unable to get the medical attention they rely on in order to provide for themselves and their families. We pray for them and their families. We pray that jobs will be restored to their previous levels, or that the underemployed or unemployed would soon find suitable, steady work in healthy, positive work environments where they are valuable contributors to the success of their company. May they work heartily for You, Lord, rather than just to man. We pray they will not lose their faith and will turn to You in these difficult times. Lord, You promise if we seek Your kingdom and know You as our righteousness, You will give us each and every day what we need no matter what the circumstances (Matt. 6:25-34).

We pray for employers that their business will remain profitable, so they can pay their employees and add more to their workforce. We pray for the supply chains: the farmers, truckers, meatpackers, grocers, warehouse people, etc... Keep the goods and services open, available and coming, Lord. We pray there are no shortages that cause hoarding, hardships, or unemployment. We have come to heavily rely on these services and suppliers to meet our needs and to conduct business.

Oh, Lord, we pray for supernatural wisdom for our leaders in making wise decisions in directing our economy. We pray for leaders who will look to You for wisdom and use biblical guidelines in the many challenges they deal with and decide on. Lord, You have clear vision of the days ahead. Help us trust and rest in what You have for us. Thank you, Father, that You are the Creator of the universe and that You hear and answer our prayers according to Your will. In Jesus' name, Amen

Day 12

Law Enforcement

Numbers 10:9   *When you go to war in your land against the enemy who oppresses you, then you shall sound an alarm with the trumpets, and you will be remembered before the Lord your God, and you will be saved from your enemies.*

Deuteronomy 31:6   *Be strong and of good courage, do not fear nor be afraid of them; for the Lord your God, He is the One who goes with you. He will not leave you nor forsake you.*

PRAYER:

Father, we call out for Your help and protection of our men and women who are on the frontline of battle: our law enforcement officers. These men and women stand between us and chaos, between law and order, and crime. They put their lives on the line for our safety and freedoms.

Our nation is in confusion. The precepts of right and wrong are being questioned, replaced with a shift toward tolerance and intolerance. In some cities, our mayors, city councilors and state legislators have taken measures to defund or even eliminate police departments. These steps restrict or remove some basic abilities designed to protect us and stop crime. Some in authority are enacting budgets and laws which seem to open the gate for tyranny and terrorism to reign, giving way to anarchy, mayhem and corruption. In some places in our beautiful country, criminals are being left unchallenged to roam our communities and repeat their offenses. This is an unconscionable sin against our people. We are aware that both Hitler and Mussolini removed the police. History reveals what happened. Lord, we must not forget! We must not repeat the wrongs! Father, forgive our legislators for making dangerous, politically-driven moves that lead to a destabilization of our communities and our nation. Indeed, the speed at which this is happening makes it appear like it is a scheme of the enemy. It seems that our law makers – many of them willingly - are playing right into the enemy's hand. Lord, remove the stain of this sin over our cities and let righteousness flow like a river. Let wisdom, law and order prevail.

The men and women in law enforcement are here to protect all lives; black, white, red and yellow; men and women; young and old. All people are precious in Your sight. We pray for godly wisdom, discernment and justice to be upon those who dedicate their lives to protect our people, so they may do what is right in Your sight. We pray for them as David prayed for Solomon in 1 Kings 2:3: "And keep the charge of the Lord your God: to walk in His ways, to keep His statutes, His commandments, His judgments, and His testimonies". Help Christians in law enforcement lead with wisdom and influence one another in righteousness and courage.

We pray that law enforcement leadership would unconditionally support just and righteousness protocol and procedures. In Jesus' name, we pray for Your hedge of protection over these men and women, and for protection from false accusations based on political correctness. We pray for their families' protection.

We pray that our police, sheriff, National Guard and other military branches would discern the schemes of the enemy as it pertains to domestic and foreign terrorism. Give them the insight, protection and boldness needed to detect their schemes and to go forth into the enemy's camp. Lord, sever the ties of corrupt companionship in people and organizations. Bring evil-doers and terrorists to the saving knowledge of Jesus Christ. May they truly repent of their sin and turn from their wicked ways. Provide these new believers a way of escape from the path of wickedness, darkness and despair. We pray that every terrorist cell would destruct from within, and that they would have utterly failed leadership, failed communication and that every attempt of evil would be thwarted as in 2 Chron 20. Unless You go into battle before us, we dare not go, for You, oh Lord, are mighty in battle, and You are righteous!

We pray for a God-honoring unity in the military leadership of our nation, in the White House and in congress. Lord, let the United States - 'one nation under God' - continue to be a beacon of freedom and liberty for all. Lord, let it be so again! In Jesus' Name.

I now pray especially for those I know who serve our people: _____ and for the men, women and their families who serve. I pray for those in authority who make laws in my community to rise up and take a stand for righteousness based on Your principles. Help them stand strong, even go against the flow of political correctness. Bless those who take a stand for righteousness with the people's favor and Your favor, Lord. In Jesus Name, Amen

Day 13

Government in Recovery

1 Timothy 2:2 ... *for kings and all who are in authority, that we may lead a quiet and peaceable life in all godliness and reverence.*

Isaiah 61:4 *And they shall rebuild the old ruins, they shall raise up the former desolations, and they shall repair the ruined cities, the desolations of many generations.*

Prayer:

Merciful and loving God we implore You to come to our aid. We pray for the wisdom we need to guide our community, state, nation, world and our people through our current crisis. Bring us to an enlightened place where the poor are protected, our laws are just and merciful, our basic needs are provided for and where hope reigns in our hearts.

Bring blessing and strength through Your hand to all who serve in our communities and nation: mayors, city councilors, county commissioners, police chiefs, judges, governors, cabinet members and to our Presidential leadership. Help all who work to maintain and safeguard the quality of life that we enjoy and are blessed with. Sustain all who bring security to our lives. Keep their hearts turned toward You as they serve.

Lord, as a nation, we have witnessed serious challenges, confusion and some disastrous choices in government spending and decision making. Our leaders are being inundated with information, some of it true, and some not. We ask for a sovereign move of Your Holy Spirit to bring practical, efficient discernment to solving problems.

Help our leaders go against the flow when necessary to set things in right order between God and man. Give them courage to conquer obstacles and opposition, political pressure and oppression. Help them budget and spend with wisdom and compassion for the people who will bear the tax burden. Father, when our nation has been in crisis and shut down, some state governments have been busy enacting laws that are not the voice of the people they serve. Many of these laws violate Your precepts. We stand in the gap and plead, "forgive, Abba, Father!" Wash away our state and national sin with Your precious blood. Help us walk in forgiveness towards them, while respecting and holding our leaders up in prayer. Our people, our state and nation are desperate for Your hand of redemption to undo works of darkness.

Lord, we ask for a special level of wisdom and understanding for all leadership, community, county, state and national to make excellent choices and guidance to get us back on track with a thriving economy following the coronavirus. We ask that our legislators would take a protective leadership role to protect our cities, state and nation from community violence. We pray they would support our police officers as they put their lives on the line for us. Equip them to restore godly order in our streets and cities.

Jesus was born and raised in a small town, grew up under the authority of small-town life. When He walked with us on this earth, He spread His healing power. Help our elected officials and government to act with this same loving, self-less character. Help them use their offices and power to protect, support and promote the well-being of all people.

Keep us strong in faith and love. Through Christ our Lord. Amen.

Day 14

Families & Social Services in Recovery

Ephesians 3:14-21 *[14] For this reason I bow my knees to the Father of our Lord Jesus Christ, [15] from whom the whole family in heaven and earth is named, [16] that He would grant you, according to the riches of His glory, to be strengthened with might through His Spirit in the inner man, [17] that Christ may dwell in your hearts through faith; that you, being rooted and grounded in love, [18] may be able to comprehend with all the saints what is the width and length and depth and height— [19] to know the love of Christ which passes knowledge; that you may be filled with all the fullness of God. [20] Now to Him who is able to do exceedingly abundantly above all that we ask or think, according to the power that works in us, [21] to Him be glory in the church by Christ Jesus to all generations, forever and ever. Amen.*

Prayer:

Our Heavenly Father, throughout your Word and in Your dealings with the people of the earth, You have both spoken and demonstrated Your deep love and protection for families, marriages, and children. We know that You have established righteous structures and patterns for families that, when lived out in humility through You and before You, give fathers and mothers the means to directly reflect Your great love to their children, even in the midst of these difficult days. And, Father, we recognize that, in our human frailty and sin, we have fallen short of these ideals both in our homes and in our country, often leaving our children, and the children in our midst, with emotional and spiritual scars, doubts and anxieties.

Knowing and trusting that You are the Father of mercy and grace, the One true healer and restorer, we come in humility, repenting and asking, in the name of Jesus, for forgiveness for any and all pain our sin and shortcomings have caused within our own families, and for the sin of the people of our nation. We ask too, that in Your mercy You will heal their wounded hearts and restore to them Your promised peace *"which surpasses all understanding,"* to *"guard their hearts and minds through Christ Jesus."* (Philippians 4:7)

As we look beyond our own families, Father, we recognize that many families, locally and across the nation, have been emotionally and spiritually traumatized in these past several months by financial diffi-culties, the upheaval of our social structure, and the anxieties of an uncertain future. And, Father, we have been made aware of the spike in domestic violence within homes across our land, causing even greater wounding and distress. We know, Father, that these things break your heart, and that Your Word tells us that You hold a special place for those who are weak and vulnerable. You, indeed are, *"A father of the fatherless, a defender of widows,"* and that you, Lord, *"set the solitary in families,"* and *"bring out those who are bound into prosperity."* (Psalm 68:5-6)

Lastly, Lord, we acknowledge our place at the side of children and spouses who are vulnerable and lonely; that we would be the tangible hands and feet that reflect Your heart. As your servant James re-minded us, *"Pure and undefiled religion before God and the Father is this: to visit orphans and widows in their trouble, and to keep one-self unspotted from the world."* (James 1:27). We join You in Your heartache and commit ourselves to Your mercy and grace.

Father, we earnestly pray for all law enforcement and government of-ficials who are tasked with the responsibility of assessment and inter-vention for our families in crisis. We pray that Your Spirit will go before these public servants, even if they are not your followers, and that they would choose wise and righteous plans of action and resto-ration that reflect Your heart and your guidelines for children and

36

families. We pray further mercy and healing for our officials, as they are often overworked and overexposed to situations of abuse and trauma, and pray that they may find peace and relief, especially when they are tempted to sin in response.

Father God, we have violated Your principles by enacting laws that violate Your Word. We have passed laws which undermine the sanctity of life at conception and allow unborn babies to be taken up to the moment of birth by abortion. With our laws we have undermined the marriage. You have defined in Your Word between one man and one woman, and as a state and nation, we have caused, perpetuated and funded extreme gender confusion and anxiety. Father, we confess this as sin and repent for it. We need Your help to get these laws overturned. Lord, please forgive us for silently watching all this take place. Help us put godly people in positions of authority. Help advocates stand up. Help ordinary citizens take a stand, pray and write letters to convey our concerns. We ask for mercy and help. Give us strength, power, passion, and endurance to pursue Your righteousness.

We pray these things in Jesus' name,
Amen

Day 15

Education System Recovery

Deuteronomy 6:6-7 "*And these words which I command you today shall be in your heart.* ⁷ *You shall teach them diligently to your children, and shall talk of them when you sit in your house, when you walk by the way, when you lie down, and when you rise up.*

Proverbs 2: 1-6 *My son, if you receive my words,*
And treasure my commands within you,
² *So that you incline your ear to wisdom,*
And apply your heart to understanding;
³ *Yes, if you cry out for discernment,*
And lift up your voice for understanding,
⁴ *If you seek her as silver,*
And search for her as for hidden treasures;
⁵ *Then you will understand the fear of the LORD,*
And find the knowledge of God.
⁶ *For the LORD gives wisdom;*
From His mouth come knowledge and understanding;

Prayer:

Father we come to You as Your children, seeking Your ways in our times. The coronavirus has forced a "reset" in the way we do school. We ask that You use this reset to accomplish Your purposes. We lift up our school systems as they grapple with how to re-engage the schools and how to re-integrate children and adults back into classrooms, from pre-school to colleges. Help our administrators and teachers come up with creative ideas for every need. Give them divine wisdom and ideas for how to connect with each student. Strengthen and give endurance to our teachers to fight the good fight of faith. Help them notice students that are failing to engage in online school or in the classroom. Let the teachers have tenacity to advocate for students whose home situation is unstable. We pray for an extra measure of grace for these teachers and students and for godly order in each home. Give teachers creativity and skills to keep the students focused when doing their computer classes. We release the love of the Father to work through these teachers to give the students a vision and a hope. Help the students to be authors and finishers of their schoolwork. Give them a heart to achieve and do schoolwork as unto You with a spirit of excellence. In Jesus' name, we ask for practical strategies to overcome educational hurdles for school systems, teachers, parents and students. Help each child accomplish educational goals even though their school year was disrupted.

We pray for parents who are not actively involved with their children's schoolwork, that they would take an interest and be a part of providing reinforcement at home. Let this year be a starting point of new parental engagement and support of students and teachers to accomplish educational goals. Lord, we ask for resources for parents to be good stewards with their children …for love, food, shelter, time, value, stability, supervision and discipline and to take this responsibility seriously.

We know that Your Son Jesus is the Way, the Truth and the Life; the Light of the world! Thank You for giving us children, and the opportunity of raising the next generation to godliness and good works. As a society, we repent of going our own way, for allowing ungodly cultural ideologies to direct the educational flow, of not looking out for the needs of others, for considering what we know to be more important than who we are. As parents, we repent for being disengaged in our children's education when we are needed. We ask for an education system for all the people that supports seeking Your true wisdom, knowledge and understanding and love for one another.

Thank you, Father, that You are doing a new thing, giving us new ideas, and providing creative, innovative and personalized ways for each student to reach the full potential You created for them. In Jesus Name, Amen

Your Word has given parents the responsibility for educating their children. Therefore, we also ask for and pray into these things:

- An educational system aligned to support the responsibility of parents for their children.
- An educational system that would not take the place, supplant, contradict, or negate the authority of the parents in any way, but work to support each family in raising, nurturing, and educating their children.
- A new understanding of public schools' funding, practice and purpose.
- An explosion of options for our families to be created.
- The opportunity for all families to be able to choose the educational option that best fits their child's need.
- Godly educational systems to arise and be found excellent. That in that excellence any family that would desire to have their children benefit would be allowed to do so.
- The location of residence or funding no longer be a barrier to school choice.
- True wisdom is provided to discern what is the responsibility of the state and what is the responsibility of the church and family. And that separation of these two entities be based on love and respect, not fear.
- The core of our educational system be centered on the child and their development as mature adults, able to discern right from wrong, growing in wisdom.

Day 16

Education Curriculum

Proverbs 1:7   The fear of the Lord is the beginning of knowledge, but fools despise wisdom and instruction.

2 Tim. 3:16-18   All scripture is given by inspiration of God, and is profitable for doctrine, for reproof, for correction, for instruction in righteousness, that the man of God may be complete, thoroughly equipped for every good work.

Col. 3:16   Let the word of Christ dwell in you richly in all wisdom, teaching and admonishing one another in psalms and hymns and spiritual songs, singing with grace in your hearts to the Lord.

PRAYER:

Dear Heavenly Father, You honor teachers as one of the pillars of the Christian community. In fact, one of the many names of your Son Jesus was that of Teacher. He taught the disciples, the disciples passed down His teachings to the new followers, and so on. We are so glad that there were teachers to share the story of how You loved us so much that You sent Your Son to save us from our sins!

However, times are so different nowadays. Our children attend public schools that do not permit any knowledge of You to be mentioned. At its core, the curriculum is human-centered, not God-centered. Many theories are taught as facts with no discussion allowed. Too much time in the classroom is spent on material that is not relevant or proper and not enough time on basic skills. We have a nation of children and young adults who cannot spell or write a coherent sentence.

Oh Lord, we pray for changes in the classroom. We pray that teachers would no longer teach subject matter that should instead be taught by parents at home. We pray that parents would be allowed to have a voice on the educational materials used in the classroom and that these are age appropriate. We pray that our children are also taught to be good citizens, that they learn the accurate history of this country and study the foundational documents that make it so exceptional. We need our children to have a strong foundation to develop into caring, well-rounded and intelligent adults.

Lord God, we lift up our school boards and curriculum administrators. Please give them wisdom and sensitivity to make excellent choices in the material they acquire. Open their eyes and hearts to the true needs of our students. Have them turn to You and Your Word as their guide. We ask that associations, which operate teacher's unions, would have a correction in the direction they push their social agendas. We ask for wisdom as a nation to know how to undo the works of darkness which have been funneled through these organizations. Raise up Your champions to oppose and overcome these strategies. Father, we need Your help. You are mighty in battle.   In Jesus' name we pray.

Day 17

Media

2 Chronicles 14:11 *And Asa cried out to the LORD his God, and said, "LORD, it is nothing for You to help, whether with many or with those who have no power; help us, O LORD our God, for we rest on You, and in Your name we go against this multitude. O LORD, You are our God; do not let man prevail against You!"*

Psalm 103:19 *The Lord has established His throne in heaven, and His kingdom rules over all.*

Isaiah. 45:6 *That they may know from the rising of the sun to its setting That there is none besides Me. I am the LORD, and there is no other;*

Prayer:
Holy, just and merciful Father, we praise You. Thank You that You are the all-powerful Ruler and sustainer of all things; the giver of all that is good. You are the author of love, peace, salvation. You alone are God. There is no other. Is. 45 and Psalm 103:19.

Father, we lift up the media in all of its broad and varied formats: tv, radio, newspaper, internet, social media platforms, movies, entertainment, etc.. Today, we live 24/7 subjected to some form of the media. We are influenced by it, conditioned and cultured by it. We have been entertained, informed, and now left aghast as our beliefs, perspectives and emotions are impacted by the realities or distortions of what we see, hear, read, or interact with. Lord, increasingly, we are being pressured how to think, what to believe, how to decipher right or wrong. We are told what our perspectives, values and morals should be.

Some would call this political or societal propaganda: "a deceptive, distorted information system to promote a policy, idea or cause."

A single news story, tweet, or social post can and does influence hundreds of millions each day. More and more, we are aware of the internet moguls' gate-keeping control and manipulation of actual or fake news with what is allowed or taken down online.

Lord, we are appalled at evil masquerading as good; at unjust, false narratives. One-sided opinions versus non-biased objective reporting. We are grieved at the depravity promoted in our media: unloving, evil, violence and hateful behaviors promoted as entertainment; demonic agendas and lies on news and talk shows. We watch people emulate wicked behaviors they see online and in the media. Forgive us for being entertained or for purchasing, watching or listening to media which makes a mockery of You and Your principles.

We are seeing unspeakable acts of violence, anarchy and property destruction being left unchallenged. We see law enforcement officers being forced to retreat in the face of angry, violent protesters.

Lord, we beg You to intervene according to Your holy will. Stop the crime, chaos and destruction. Expose those who perpetrate and promote evil of all forms through media formats. Thwart the evil influence they exert with their money and power. Demolish every evil plan and thing hidden in the darkness that is raised against You, Your laws and commands. Break the strongholds of principalities in the heavenly and physical realms that wage war against You in our country and the world (Eph 6:12). Expose these for what they are and for all to see: divisive evil political plans against the President of the United States, falsehoods and agendas against Your church, the sanctity of the family, sexuality, and the unborn. Expose, inhibit and reverse evil campaigns and political agendas of media companies who seek to influence the people of our nation for their own ungodly agendas. Lord, we are reminded of what You say in Romans 1:18-32: [18] For the wrath of God is revealed from heaven against all ungodliness and unrighteousness of men, who suppress the truth in unrighteousness... and [21] because, although they knew God, they did not glorify Him as God, nor were thankful, but became futile in their thoughts, and their foolish hearts were darkened. Professing to be wise, they became fools....

Lord, cleanse our land. Reset our media industry. Protect our nation. Break through into the hearts of the influential who control the media. Cause the fear of the Lord to be magnified in them. Bring these, who are in positions of great power and control, to saving knowledge of You and into Your kingdom for eternity. Send your Holy Spirit throughout this broad, wealthy and powerful industry to enlighten and regenerate it, all to the glory of Jesus. Reset dark minds with Holy-Spirit inspired light, goodness and truth. Give those in the media eyes to see, ears to hear, and hearts to discern and choose good over evil. Set this industry in a new direction so that it operates according to Your will and is blessed by You. You are the only One who can bring good out of this. We cry out to You for Your touch. Save our nation, founded 'one nation under God.'

Lord, I don't want to be stuck or immobilized by worry, anxiety or fear. Help me pray for those who act as enemies of Jesus and the gospel through the media. I ask you to give me a spirit of calm, assurance, and strength. You are in control. You reign over all that is good. You have power over all that is evil. I rest in this. I have the privilege of meditating on You, on Your word. Not on the world, the media or worries. You are always with me to instruct me, comfort me when I meditate on You. You will never leave me or forsake me. Deut. 31:6 I want to be as close to You as I can be. Draw me close and work in me, Holy Spirit (Jn 14, 16), according to Your will. Cause me to be a light for You, Lord.

We lift up the Christians in the media and ask for a solid hedge of protection around them. Give them strength and wisdom to resist the tide and to stand for what is right. Grant them favor. Raise up Christian champions who have the toughness to break through these strongholds with Your help, Lord. Holy Spirit transform the media of the United States and beyond.

In Jesus our Savior's name we pray, Amen.

Day 18

A Reset for Arts & Entertainment

Scripture:

John 1:1-5 *"In the beginning was the Word, and the Word was with God, and the Word was God. He was in the beginning with God. All things were made through Him, and without Him nothing was made that was made. In Him was life, and the life was the light of men. And the light shines in the darkness, and the darkness did not comprehend it."*

Philippians 4:8 *Finally, brethren, whatever things are true, whatever things are noble, whatever things are just, whatever things are pure, whatever things are lovely, whatever things are of good report, if there is any virtue and if there is anything praiseworthy—meditate on these things.*

Prayer:

Lord, today we pray for Your light to come to Hollywood and every part of the arts and entertainment arena. We know, Lord, that the arts and entertainment industry can be used mightily for Your glory! We pray that You would make a way so that thousands in this industry will come to You and confess the name of Jesus as their Savior and Lord. We thank You for those who know You who are standing up for Your name right now and who bring Your Word to television, movies, radio, the internet, and social media platforms. Guide and bless these men and women in Your truth, in their endeavors, and lead them in Your righteous ways. Inspire them and bless their creativity in ways that direct and draw people's hearts to You. We thank you for family-friendly and inspirational entertainment that warms our hearts. Strengthen those who produce these and help them to continue going against the flow!

Lord, we pray for the dark side of Hollywood. We come before Your throne of grace to find help for an industry which has capitalized on the promotion of evil agendas: witchcraft, occult, extreme violence, murder, horror, terror, pornography, child pornography; rampant degradation of societal norms, promotion of promiscuity, political coercion, division, bigotry, mockery of Your name, profanity, Anti-Christian and anti-American propaganda, etc. Our people have seen and heard things that violate Your word in every sense. We have become desensitized or addicted to violence. Some escape into fantasy - video games. We have lost control over what our children watch, and innocence and purity has been eroded, lost. Some have retreated into a sedentary, isolated culture and do not know You. For many this entertainment arena has become their god. Father, we as Your people confess to have partaken and been entertained by this. We have watched it and shrugged our shoulders. Wickedness has been made casual through this powerful form of communication. Lord, as intercessors, we come like David did in the face of Goliath. Our smooth stone is called, "Repentance". We confess these sins as wickedness. Cleanse our hearts and minds from the images. Turn our hearts toward pure and holy things. Lord, forgive us for allowing this industry to shape our lives and thinking.

We lift up those in control of the arts and entertainment industry who have purposely created a platform in which they can control the direction of culture with great expertise. We ask that there would be no money in it, or bankruptcy for the ones creating wicked, demonically driven programming. We pray that those at the top of the arts and entertainment 'mountain' would have a "Come to Jesus" moment; that they would realize they have blood on their hands. Cleanse them with Your blood and turn their hearts away from greed, evil and cultural control. Bring them in humility to Your throne of grace to find help. They are Your creation... Your children who have gone astray. We cry out for You to touch their hearts. Let them use their great resources and skills to reach a hurting world for You, to bring hope, and restoration. We ask You to forgive us for watching, for funding an industry that promotes violence, occultic activity, and perversions of every kind. Help us identify and support Christian works. We pray protection over all Christian programming, magazines, on-line, social media, and ask that they be sovereignly protected and operated by biblical principles. Guard them against selling out to political agendas or propaganda brought about by interest groups. Lord, may Americans bless wholesome family entertainment that strengthens our culture with love, unity, encouragement, and inspiration. Let those companies that advocate for biblical family values as identified in Your Word, flourish. Lord, send Your angels to do Your bidding and grant them favor with financing.

We pray that Your light would shine into and permeate every area of the arts and entertainment industry - dark places which Satan uses to kill, steal and destroy. These may be likened to modern day 'high places'. May they be taken down in Jesus' name.
Let our arts and entertainment be on Earth as it is in heaven! In Jesus Name, Amen!

Day 19

Godly Leadership in the Seven Mountains

Scripture:

Exodus 18:19-21 *Stand before God for the people, so that you may bring the difficulties to God.* *²⁰ And you shall teach them the statutes and the laws and show them the way in which they must walk and the work they must do.* *²¹ Moreover you shall select from all the people able men, such as fear God, men of truth, hating covetousness; and place such over them to be rulers of thousands, rulers of hundreds, rulers of fifties, and rulers of tens.*

Ps 89:14 *Righteousness and justice are the foundation of your throne*

Prayer:

Heavenly Father, we come boldly to Your throne of grace to ask for help in our time of need. Oh, how we need you in this time of great shaking in our nation. May your perfect will be done in the midst of these trials, as old wineskins are being replaced with new.

We pray blessings over what some have termed the 'seven mountains' of societal influence that shape our culture. We come in humility and ask forgiveness for allowing the world, the flesh and the devil to infiltrate these and other areas. We ask You to heal our land. We pray for kingdom-minded people to rise up and take positions of authority and influence in each of these areas:

Government/Military/Police

Media

Arts and Entertainment

Business

Education
Religion
Family

Father, we pray for those in leadership at every level in these 'mountains' to have divine wisdom, strength, and endurance. We pray they would honor You. Grant them the ability to articulate a godly vision and strategy. Touch a coal to their lips. Strengthen them to build godly teams. Create kind, strong, healthy relationships that are without manipulation or intimidation and grant them favor and influence. Help them consistently overcome evil with good! Raise them to the top. Help each leader to resist the evil one. We ask for a repeated tidal wave of revival to go through every cultural 'mountain'. We ask that You remove those who will not honor You. We ask You to remove those who have trained to bring chaos, division and strife. Send them to where they will not be able to cause damage, and where they will find You. We release God-inspired understanding and visions to be birthed in leader's hearts. Give them clarity to know how to turn things around and bring restoration to broken management. Lord, at the top of our 'mountains', there is deep darkness. There are roots of spiritual wickedness that bring defilement to our land. We repent for the political correctness and agendas that are being forced on every part of all these 'mountains'. We ask that You wash us with Your precious blood, removing the constant stain of sin. We cry out for You to break the yoke of bondage over every 'mountain', every sin that has entangled. Give the stamina to godly leaders to run the race with endurance that You have set before them, looking to You, the author and finisher of their faith. Lord, raise up teams of intercessors to pray through the strongholds of each 'mountain'. You are the Alpha & Omega. You have ALL power and authority. We thank You, for taking back the reins.

We ask for a spirit of wisdom and revelation upon the heads of our governing authorities, military and police. *'Surround them with favor as a shield.' Psalm 5:12.* We pray for truth that sets free in the mountain of media, and ask that individuals be held accountable for intentional lies and distortions of truth.

Lord, war is raging in the arts and entertainment arena. Christians are mocked and slandered, history is rewritten, and perversion is celebrated. We say, 'no' to this and pray for righteousness to be restored. We pray for men and women of faith to rise to the top in business. We pray that they would recognize their calling to speak boldly for truth and to make righteous decisions. Give them godly advisors and great courage to stand up against persuasions of unbiblical political correctness.

We pray, Father, that You would be invited - welcomed - back into our schools; that godly values stemming from Your truth would be a part of every subject, every curriculum. We pray that teachers and administrators would possess a spirit of excellence; that they would speak wisdom, hope and life into the generations. We pray for religious liberty in America and for Your church to speak uncompromised truth in love. We ask for a great and imminent revival in our nation, which also leads to reformation in the leadership of these 'mountains' according to Your will.

Oh, Lord, how You love family. It is under assault. We pray blessings over families. We pray fathers would take their place as leaders in the home, and children would be taught of the Lord. We declare marriage between one man and one woman would be the honored by all and ask that marriages be strengthened and healed.

Heavenly Father, thank You for this great nation. We pray it would once again be a beacon of light to the nations of the world, so that '*the earth would be filled with the knowledge of the glory of the Lord, as the waters cover the sea.*' *Hab 2:14* In Jesus strong name, Amen.

Day 20

The Prodigal Nation

Luke 15:13,18-21,24 And not many days after, the younger son (nation) gathered all together, journeyed to a far country (away from the Lord), and there wasted his possessions with prodigal living. [18] I will arise and go to my father, and will say to him, "Father, I have sinned against heaven and before you, [19] and I am no longer worthy to be called your son. Make me like one of your hired servants." [20] "And he arose and came to his father. But when he was still a great way off, his father saw him and had compassion, and ran and fell on his neck and kissed him. [21] And the son said to him, 'Father, I (America) have sinned against heaven and in your sight and am no longer worthy to be called your son (nation).... [24] for this my son (nation) was dead and is alive again; he was lost and is found.' And they began to be merry.
–Paraphrased for the nation

Exhortation:

America, how far you have gone from your first love. This nation was built on the Gospels and God's Law and Principles. Many lives have died defending what God has given to us. Like the Prodigal Son, America has left her first love. America has wasted her inheritance in reckless and immoral living. Gone are the days when America held her head high and honored God. America removed God's Word from the schools. America has redefined marriage. America has said it is alright to kill the unborn. America has legalized drugs and prostitution in our lands. America how far you have strayed and now you are in the pig pen-- now it's time to come to your senses. It is time to acknowledge that you have sinned and call out to God in repentance. Our Heavenly Father is waiting for us. HE is running to you, America, and waiting to embrace you once again. America, you will be restored once again as a great nation and a beacon of hope. As was the prodigal son, so is America. LORD, we long for the day when we can say "We once were lost but now are found. It is time to celebrate."

Father, we are fully aware that we have become a prodigal nation. We have squandered the foundation laid by our forefathers; a nation established on Your precepts. We have fallen with immorality, perversion, broken covenants and innocent blood shed. As a nation, we have called good things bad and bad things good. We have violated Your Commandments in every possible way. We have failed to revere and honor You. We have become adulterous in our way with many idols which we have placed before You. Your Word states that, IF Your people will humble themselves, repent, and turn from their wicked ways, You will hear us from heaven. Lord, we do this on behalf of our nation. We are grieved over the decisions and laws that we, the people, have established, that violate You. We are grieved when we don't stand up and resist unrighteousness as a nation. We are grieved to think that in our wickedness, You would turn Your face from us. We cry out to You, for forgiveness and to have mercy on us, Lord. We are desperate for our nation to turn its heart back toward You. We pray that every aspect of the way we function would honor You and Your precepts, in every sphere of influence from our Churches, Governments, Media, Families, Military and Law Enforcement, arts and entertainment. We are in great need of a move of Your Holy Spirit to blow across our land, turning every heart, bringing us back to You, Your wholesomeness, and hope. Thank You for Your mercy and love, which will never leave us nor forsake us. Turn our nation's heart back toward You! We thank You, that even while we are far off, You will run to us. Your Love fails not!

Lord, help me to live my own life in a way that glorifies You. When I am going astray, help me turn and run back toward You, with the knowledge that You are coming to meet me. Help me to love my country enough to pray for it. I need courage to speak up and take a stand for Your righteousness. Show me where I need to honor You -- in every area of my life -- with love and courage. You are a BIG God and You are running to meet me! I need You, and my nation needs You, desperately. In Jesus Name! Amen.

Day 21

Restoration of a Nation Divided

Proverbs 14:34   *Righteousness exalts a nation, but sin is a reproach to any people.*

Psalms 33:12   *Blessed is the nation whose God is the Lord, ...*

Psalms 133:1,3   *Behold, how good and how pleasant it is for brethren to dwell together in unity! ... For there the Lord commanded the blessing— Life forevermore.*

2 Chronicles 7:14, Jeremiah 18:8

PRAYER:
Dear Lord, our Heavenly Father,

Our nation is in need of an awakening to Your ways! Your Word says that righteousness will exalt a nation. So, we ask for the hearts of our leaders to be open to your wisdom and ways. We are asking for Your divine intervention to heal our land and that righteous judgments and decisions are made by our government and court system. We ask that honesty and truth would be restored to our culture and very fabric of our society.

Lord, we are grieved by the conduct of our leaders and people as they denounce one another and refuse to work toward the common good of the people. There has been a spirit of division amongst our leaders and people. Your Word says, a nation divided against itself cannot stand. Forgive us Lord! Bring our leaders, regardless of their party, to come together in peace, to work together at re-building the nation we love, to strengthen our infra-structure, to rebuild our military, and to care for our people. Let our leaders and our people put aside their philosophies, pride and pettiness, and seek the higher path of reconciliation. Lord, You, are the Restorer of the breach, and without You, working in each person, we cannot do this. We cry out to You to heal every division and every faction.

We are asking for the unity that is needed to incur Your blessing! Lord, Your Word says that "Blessed is the nation whose God is the Lord." We pray for all those in authority at every level of government – Federal, State and Local. We ask for the Holy Spirit to heal the great division we see in our nation. The clash between Biblical values and ungodly philosophical values, indeed the clash between light and darkness, is a huge reason for this incredible division. But Your Word says, Woe to those who call evil good, and good evil; Who put darkness for light, and light for darkness; but it also says, "I will make darkness light before them, and crooked places straight …For it is God who commanded light to shine out of darkness. These things I will do for them, and not forsake them. Nothing is impossible with You, Lord! So, we pray that there would be a great opening of Your Word in their hearts, that they would be able to experience the joy of salvation. Father, as your people, we purpose to humble ourselves before you and turn from our own selfish ways, that You would forgive our sin and heal our land. We desperately need Your help to do this.

*Lord, if there is any divisive way in me, expose it. I am listening. _____Let the words of my heart and mouth be words of reconciliation and hope. For out of the abundance of my heart, my mouth speaks. Lord, I purpose to build unity and hope in my life, in those around me, in my church and in my country, and especially unity with You. In Jesus name I pray, Amen!

Day 22

Expose and Overcome the Dark Agendas with Your Light

Scripture:

Ephesians 5:8-11, *For you were once in darkness, but now you are light in the Lord. Walk as children of light for the fruit of the Spirit is in all goodness, righteousness and truth, finding out what is acceptable to the Lord. And have no fellowship with unfruitful works of darkness, but rather expose them.*

Luke 8:16-17, *No one when he has lit a lamp, covers it with a vessel or puts it under a bed, but sets it on a lampstand, that those who enter may see the light. For nothing is secret that will not be revealed nor anything hidden that will not be known and come to light.*

Isaiah 60:1-2, *Arise, shine; For your light has come! And the glory of the Lord is risen upon you. For behold, the darkness shall cover the earth, and deep darkness the people; But the Lord will arise over you, and His glory will be seen upon you.*

Prayer:

Heavenly Father, we praise Your name above all names. Hear our prayers. We praise You as our Creator, Redeemer, our holy and majestic Father of all life, truth and light. Your word says, 'You are light and in You there is no darkness at all'. (John 1:5) Lord, we humble ourselves as we come to Your throne of mercy and grace. Thank you, Lord. We are truly grateful for Your mercy and our salvation through the shed blood of your son Jesus Christ.

Much of our nation, founded on Your laws and precepts and by people who were called by Your name, is now in deep darkness. Father, forgive us for allowing Your name and Your ways to be removed from important institutions in the land, especially in parts of the education system, media, business, governing bodies and many families. Your name has been blasphemed in arts and entertainment, in our families and in the media. Father, forgive us. We have spilled blood of more than 60 million innocent babies, endorsed by ungodly abortion laws. Our people even pay for this with taxes. Our hearts grieve…we cry out, forgive us! Cover the stain of our sin and help us make our laws righteous. Behind closed doors, laws are being set in motion which violate many of Your precepts. Our land has been defiled and we cry out for the washing of our nation by Your precious blood, for the healing of our nation.

We, the Church, repent for having been lukewarm instead of resolute when we should have stood strong for Your righteousness and Word. We come now as the darkness is growing intolerable. Lord we grapple with immorality, degradation and corruption in our society, in our cities and on our streets. We know that principalities and powers and rulers in darkness of the age (Eph. 6:12) are prompting evil doers and the unscrupulous leaders to enact laws behind closed doors. This hidden and deceptive lawmaking brings pain and suffering to the people in all manner of social, financial and cultural ways. Dark agendas defile our legislative process in the nation and in many states, including our own. We know that some people of wealth and power support and promote violence and unrest, and that many lawmakers and leaders join in this entrapment while the country's eyes are diverted and distracted with COVID-19 virus. Intentional lies twist and distort truth to undermine general goodwill, trust in our history and in one another. Lord, expose these evil doers, lawmakers and unjust laws. Expose the agendas and the people that desire to bring down our great nation.

Bring into the light the corruption and lust for power behind it. Lord, we cry out for Your light and Your truth to prevail in our nation. We cry out for Your true justice to prevail. So we speak to these mountains of corruption, "Be thou removed and cast into the sea of justice and mercy."

In prayer, we cry as one that Your Holy Spirit be strong in each member of Your body and that we rise as one, fervent in prayer and Your love. Lord, let us arise in and as Your light to overcome the darkness and corruption in our nation. Let us bring those that are deceived into the light of your Son, Jesus Christ.

In action, move upon Your people to rise up, to speak boldly in love in the marketplace and in places of authority, to overcome evil with good. Lord, we need godly leadership in every sphere of our culture. Speak to Your people, to wake up, rise up, and be of very good courage. Help Your people possess the promised land. Fill their mouths with the Word of God, and when they speak, grant them favor with You and with man. During this season of elections, we cry out that those with dark agendas, impractical, unaffordable plans be replaced with godly leaders who can lead with wisdom, strength and who can put our communities, state and nation back on track with Your purposes.

Lord, we cry out once again. Make us that 'one nation under God' this was our foundation from You. Lord, once again let us be the salt and light, the city on a hill and beacon of hope for the masses that You intended. Lord, empower us with Your love and wisdom to restore and transform America to the destiny You have planned.
In Christ's name we pray. Amen

Day 23

Healing of National Divisions & Factions

Proverbs 6:16-19 [16]*These six things the LORD hates, yes, seven are an abomination to Him;* [17]*A proud look, a lying tongue, hands that shed innocent blood,* [18]*a heart that devises wicked plans, feet that are swift to run to evil,* [19]*a false witness who speaks lies, and one who sows discord among brethren.*

Proverbs 10:12 [12]*Hatred stirs up strife, but love covers all sins.*

Matthew 5:9 [9]*Blessed are the peacemakers, for they shall be called sons of God.*

PRAYER:

Father, forgive us for entertaining a spirit of control and greed in this country. We have been divided in our expectations for the distribution of wealth by the marketplace and by our government. We have not taken responsibility for our own actions and have not sought You as our provider. You have always blessed our country with abundance. But instead of thanking You and seeking You, we have sought our own control and greed. Forgive us for envy and covetousness. We have harbored hatred and resentment for those we accuse of exploiting us and come against them with a spirit of condemnation. Forgive us for belittling and demeaning those with whom we disagree and not coming in the spirit of reconciliation. We repent of our not loving those that we perceive as our enemies and not seeking peace.

Father, as You have forgiven us, we forgive others. "But God demonstrates His own love toward us, in that while we were still sinners, Christ died for us." (Romans 5:8) We commit ourselves to showing the same love that God showed us and to seeking reconciliation. "Love your enemies, do good to those who hate you, bless those who curse you, and pray for those who spitefully use you." (Luke 6:27-28) Father, we ask for Your grace that Your law of love may rule in our hearts. We commit ourselves to extend grace and mercy to others.

We are reminded that "we do not wrestle against flesh and blood, but against principalities, against powers, against the rulers of the darkness of this age, against spiritual hosts of wickedness in heavenly places." (Ephesians 6:12) Therefore, we claim the name of Jesus and plead His blood over our homes, communities, state and this nation; that the divisive strongholds will be broken. We stand against division that comes from substance abuse and contentious spirits in our families. We come against the devaluation of other human beings, including the lives of unborn children and sex trafficking. We turn from disparaging others based upon nationality, social groups, financial conditions, or race. We ask You to break the strongholds of unforgiveness and hatred. Cut off any controlling spirits based upon greed, any spirit that would diminish the freedoms that are given by You, and any spirit of arrogance that would place ourselves or any idols above Your authority. Lord, in Your grace, we commit to encouraging, lifting up and blessing others.

Lord, we purpose to respectfully and firmly stand without compromise for truth, justice, and righteousness in this land. We ask You to break division, as we stand on Your immutable truth. In Your truth, we ask Your blessing of forgiveness, healing, restoration, acceptance and adoption of the unsaved into Your family. Strengthen us and unite us in You, Lord. In Jesus Name we pray. Amen.

Day 24

Transform Confusion and Deep Darkness
with an Explosion of Light

Psalm 82

God stands in the congregation of the mighty;
He judges among the gods.
How long will you judge unjustly,
And show partiality to the wicked? Selah
Defend the poor and fatherless;
Do justice to the afflicted and needy.
Deliver the poor and needy;
Free them from the hand of the wicked.
They do not know, nor do they understand;
They walk about in darkness;
All the foundations of the earth are unstable.
I said, "You are gods,
And all of you are children of the Most High.
But you shall die like men,
And fall like one of the princes."
Arise, O God, judge the earth;
For You shall inherit all nations.

Thank you, Precious Father, for enlightening me to pray effectively in the Spirit and by Your word. I am inspired today and energized to make tremendous power available through prayer in the mighty Name of Jesus! I will not be silent! Isaiah 60 declares that the darkness will cover the earth, and deep darkness the people. But the Lord will arise over you, and His glory will be seen upon you.

Your word is true, dear Lord, and we are seeing this in our nation today. Nothing takes You by surprise! So, we say, arise and take Your place as the righteous judge of all the earth. Heavenly Father, bind the dark rulers of confusion and put an end to their mockery and evil plots. Turn their weapons of wickedness back onto themselves, piercing their pride-filled hearts until they are the helpless. They stand condemned as they are brought to trial before the Righteous Judge!

Father, Your Word declares that "the light shines in the darkness, and the darkness did not comprehend it." (Jn. 1:5) Darkness cannot gain control of light and will never be able to even touch the light. Praise the mighty Name of Jesus! We are the light of the world and have the victory over all the devil's evil works through the shed blood of Jesus and His atoning sacrifice and victory on the cross. We stand confident because You have delivered us from all the power of darkness and have brought us into the Kingdom of Your Dear Son (Col. 1:13). We have been called out of darkness into Your marvelous light. I know who I am in Christ: I am the light of the Lord because of my union with You!

Everyone practicing evil hates the light because his deeds will be exposed (Jn. 3:20) Expose them, Lord. Explode Your blinding light of truth and redemption upon this nation, O Mighty One who lives in us, as Your people take their rightful place and storm heaven with prayers and supplication for this cause!

GOD IS LIGHT AND IN HIM IS NO DARKNESS AT ALL (1Jn. 1:5). Come Holy Spirit and blast this nation with Your blinding light of truth and righteousness! In Jesus Name! Amen!

Day 25

Community Violence

Ps.55:8-10 *I would hasten my escape from the windy storm and tempest." Destroy, O Lord, and divide their tongues, for I have seen violence and strife in the city. Day and night, they go around it on its walls; Iniquity and trouble are also in the midst of it.*

Isaiah 8:9-14 *"Be shattered, O you peoples, and be broken in pieces! Give ear, all you from far countries. Gird yourselves, but be broken in pieces; Gird yourselves, but be broken in pieces. Take counsel together, but it will come to nothing; speak the word, but it will not stand for God is with us." For the LORD spoke thus to me with a strong hand, and instructed me that I should not walk in the way of this people, saying: "Do not say, 'a conspiracy,' concerning all that this people call a conspiracy, nor be afraid of their threats, nor be troubled. The LORD of hosts, Him you shall hallow; let Him be your fear, and let Him be your dread. He will be as a sanctuary...*

PRAYER:

Father, You are righteous and holy. We ask that You capture the hearts of those who do violence and who stir up strife, lies, hatred and division.

Sometimes this violence is in our homes. Sometimes it is in our communities and cities. Sometimes it is foolishness bound up in the hearts of those who want to fight and rebel. Sometimes it is between political groups. It is driven by demonic influence where doors have been opened by people to entertain evil thoughts and activities. In Jesus name, we bind the demons of hell that sow spirits of rebellion, hatred, division and discontent. Holy Spirit soften proud and haughty hearts and reveal truth to humble hearts. Lord, we ask You to thwart every

66

evil plan and bring their plans to nothing! Bring each person engaged in this evil to repentance. Deliver each from corrupt companionship. Deliver them from the effects of gangs, substance abuse, hatred, lies and depravity. Provide them a way of escape. Many of these individuals are people with deep wounds of rejection, fear, and insecurity. It is our heart that You, the Father to the fatherless, rescue and deliver them from their sin. So, where sin abounds, grace much more abounds.

Lord, the Church needs wisdom and grace to disciple and encourage these people in the way they should go. Make supportive Christians wise as serpents and gentle as doves. Help us to not grow weary in well doing because in the end we reap a harvest. We dispatch warrior and ministering angels to watch over our cities, neighborhoods, homes and churches to protect them from all harm.

Lord, we know there is neither Jew nor Greek, slave nor free in Your kingdom. We are not black or white, brown, red or yellow. We are Your children. We give no place to racism. We are not to think more highly of ourselves or our own kind (race). We repent for dishonoring others or esteeming ourselves as better. We ask You to renew a right spirit within us toward all Your creation. Every person matters to You and therefore, every life is important to us. As our Declaration of Independence says, "*We hold these truths to be self-evident, that all men are created equal, that they are endowed by their Creator with certain unalienable Rights, that among these are Life, Liberty and the pursuit of Happiness.*" Lord, we agree with this God-ordained document!

Father, there has been confusion and inconsistency among civic leaders as they respond to riots and historical monuments being torn down. We are grieved over the violence and growing anti-police sentiment.

We ask You to give wisdom to civic leaders and police departments to correct the wrongs and honor those who protect us. Give them authority to maintain law and order. Heal rifts that have developed between civic leaders and police departments in our big cities. Give our police wisdom to uncover schemes hidden in darkness. Protect our police officers from ambushes set against them. Holy Spirit lead them. Lord, we ask You to honor, bless and strengthen those who protect us.

Lord, I lift up those I know who have fallen into deep rebellion toward You and toward man. _____(Name them). I pray for a sovereign move upon their heart(s). Help me pray for them regularly. Use me to share Your love. In Jesus Name, Amen

Day 26

Intentional Political Destabilization of our Nation

Scripture:

Mark 13:7-8 *"But when you hear of wars and rumors of wars, <u>do not be troubled, for such things must happen, but the end is not yet</u>. For nation will rise against nation, and kingdom against kingdom."*

Heb 4:14-16 *"Seeing then that we have a great High Priest who has passed through the heavens, Jesus the Son of God, let us hold fast our confession…16 Let us therefore come boldly to the throne of grace, that we may obtain mercy and find grace to help in time of need."*

Psalms 89:11,13-14 *The heavens are Yours, the earth also is Yours; The world and all its fullness, … ¹³ You have a mighty arm; Strong is Your hand, and high is Your right hand. ¹⁴ Righteousness and justice are the foundation of Your throne; …*

PRAYER:

Father God, this day my heart is broken for our nation that You love--the United States of America. I am undone, and I look to You, our only answer. The flood is here, we are beyond being desperate. Our land is filled with twisted politics—hopelessness and fear now control millions. Forgive my prayerlessness regarding the daily issues we face. But I remember You said, *"<u>All things are possible to them that believe.</u>"* You said that You have extended Your scepter and even now I hear the Lion of Judah roaring! As Your child, You have given me authority, so in the mighty Name of Jesus, and in the power of the Holy Ghost--I roar also! (Proverbs 28:1) I declare according to Your

Word that above the furious flood, You, the enthroned One reigns, the King-God rules with eternity at Your side! Your justice and righteousness will be sent out as Your command to our nation, and that Your Word runs very swiftly, even now as I pray! Lord, we lift up those who are willing to stoop to the immoral and their ways, who falsify information, and who point a finger at innocence. Rampant greed and ill-gotten power are at work to establish ungodly precepts: a one world government, abortion, and the promotion of anti-Christian values. Undo ungodly, community organizing groups who train people in the systematic erosion of our Constitution and Judeo-Christian foundation. Lord, undo the 'deep state'. Expose it to the authorities who will hold them justly accountable. Cleanse the FBI, CIA, NSA and all officials and politicians who have accepted bribes, or who bribe with money or power promises (the lusts of the flesh). These are those whom we rely on for uprightness and truth. Arise, Oh Lord, and do not allow evil politicians to prevail. Let them be judged in Your sight. I roar against these evil powers of darkness in the mighty Name of Jesus, in whose Name I pray their mouths are silenced and that all attempts cease which seek to destroy and bring division our nation. Bind every evil tongue and may their lying deceitful traps snap back on them! May their foot step in their own snare.

Lord Jesus, I remember Your word and promise that says lovers of God who seek Your face can come boldly before Your throne (Hebrews 4:16). We thank You for what You are about to do! You are mighty in battle. You expose all darkness. Cause Your light to shine in the midst of the deep darkness. Help these people whom the enemy has used to come to humility, full repentance and salvation in You. God of all comfort, encourage them in the night hours to depart from

70

evil involvement. Give them courage to testify truth. Give Your angels charge over those who confess; protect and provide them with a way of escape from the bondage of evil-doing.

In the name of Jesus, I pray You send Your angels forth to do battle for Your name sake in truth, humility and righteousness against all the wiles of the enemy. May Your right-hand display awesome deeds. I decree that all things will be fulfilled only according to Your purposes and timing. By faith, I have the victory that overcomes the devil and the world. Let it be. Hallelujah!
In Jesus Name, Amen!

Day 27

For Christians to Rise Up

Psalm 1:1 *"Blessed is the man, who walks not in the counsel of the ungodly, Nor stands in the path of sinners, Nor sits in the seat of the scornful;"*

Exodus 18:21 *"Moreover you shall select from all the people able men, such as fear God, men of truth, hating covetousness; and place such over them to be rulers of thousands, rulers of hundreds, rulers of fifties, and rulers of tens."*

2 Samuel 23:3 *"...He who rules over men must be just, ruling in the fear of God."*

PRAYER:

Father, we thank You that our founding heritage as a nation is based on faith and trust in You. On our coin and currency are our guiding principles, "In God We Trust". As a nation, we enjoy the privilege, freedom and responsibility to vote as we choose. We thank You, Father, for this God-given liberty. Thank You that we can freely participate in our communities as leaders, run for elected office and that we can exercise our choice at the polls. Let us not take this for granted. Forgive us, Lord, when we have become weak or complacent when it comes to taking a stand for righteousness according to Your word. Lord, we repent and humble ourselves before You. Forgive Christians - who know Your word - for not standing up or voting. Lord, many do not vote consistent with precepts established in Your word. Forgive us for not paying attention to the decay of moral standards that now surround us. We have not only been complacent, but we have allowed the culture to shape our opinions. We have become jaded by media. We have lost sight of Your precepts that were put in place for our safety and protection. Lord, have mercy and grace upon us. Wash us with Your precious blood. Change our hearts, our minds and our faulty thinking. Help us return to the safety of Your Word which we as a nation so desperately need.

Father, we ask for righteousness to rise up in the hearts of Your people. We pray for responsible Christians who will take the time to study issues and learn about candidates who will stand for righteousness as YOU see it. Strengthen Your people with wisdom and discernment to stand up for godly values. Lord, we want to see You as King over our State, as King over the United States. Remind us of our duty to put righteous people into office and to support biblical principles in our culture. Help us place Christian voting guides into the hands of Americans. Help us say, "Yes to Life, No to unnatural death!" We yearn to do what is right in Your sight. Help Christians say, "Here am I, send me!" Raise up godly men and women in leadership roles to re-shape our culture with boldness and goodness. Give them courage and protection. Go before them and grant them favor. In Jesus Name, Amen

Day 28

Raise up a Chosen Generation - Political Candidates

Scripture:

1 Peter 2:9-10 *But you are a chosen generation, a royal priesthood, a holy nation, His own special people, that you may proclaim the praises of Him who called you out of darkness into His marvelous light; who once were not a people but are now the people of God, who had not obtained mercy but now have obtained mercy.*

Jude 16-21 *These are grumblers, complainers, walking according to their own lusts; and they mouth great swelling words, flattering people to gain advantage. But you, beloved, remember the words which were spoken before by the apostles of our Lord Jesus Christ: how they told you that there would be mockers in the last time who would walk according to their own ungodly lusts. These are sensual persons, who cause divisions, not having the Spirit.*

1 Timothy 2:1-4; Daniel 2:21; Deuteronomy 17:14-15; 17-20

Prayer:

Father, we call out to You. We have elected unrighteous judges, leaders and rulers because many of us do not vote or are not registered to vote. You have commissioned us to take a stand for righteousness, and we have sinned against our people and against You by failing to take a stand for righteousness when we don't vote. We have sinned by omission for not caring enough when we fail to do our homework on issues and candidates. Forgive us, Lord for neglecting our responsibility of taking dominion over this land You have given us and for failing to honor this God given freedom.

This nation was formed as "One Nation Under God, indivisible with liberty and justice for all." As time has gone on, Christians have acquiesced into the lie of separation of church and state by not getting involved in politics. In doing so, many ungodly men and women have filled elected positions. Unrighteous judges have been appointed by ungodly leaders or voted into office while Christian attorneys have failed to heed or answer the call of stepping up, to restore righteous order. Forgive us for allowing pressure groups and groups of activists to define a new normal. Many of these people now run unopposed for political offices. What was considered ungodly a generation ago, has become the 'normal'. We can now kill the unborn up to the moment before they are born. Our Creator no longer determines if we are male nor female, but gender is now determined by individuals. Marriage is being redefined. Forgive us Lord. These things have become law and have been upheld by our Supreme Court. We repent for jumping on the political bandwagon of the day and for making laws that dishonor or diminish Your word. We repent for allowing a party-line, which we have identified with, to overrule Your precepts.

Lord, our nation is desperate for honorable, strong leaders who uphold Your principles. Stir the hearts of men and women in every city, county, state and in the nation to answer this need with wisdom, passion and purpose. We pray that those You are calling to office will take up the mantel You have anointed them with and go forth! Let them be strong and very courageous! Let them say, "Yes and Amen," to the call. We pray You will make their way plain and straight. Season their words with truth, light and salt. Take a coal from Your alter and touch their lips with the fire of Your Holy Spirit. May Your favor fall on them. Cause them to shine with Your anointing. Help them answer questions with wisdom and truth. In debates, help them think quickly and intelligently while on their feet and speak through them wisdom as from the 'oracles of God.' When Your anointed servants speak, cause them to rise in people's favor so that listeners respond, "Yes, and Amen!" We ask for protection over them and their families, from every fiery dart the enemy tries to send their way. In righteousness they shall be established; they shall be far from oppression, for they shall not fear; and from terror, for it shall not come near them. No weapon formed against them shall prosper, and every tongue which rises against them in judgment You shall condemn.

Once elected, we pray these leaders will stay the course with You as their fore and rear guard. Let them run the race with endurance, laying aside every weight, sin and worry, looking to You, the Author and Finisher of their faith. We will pray for and support those who heed Your call. We pray that once again our nation will be 'One Nation Under God.' We pray that all eligible Christians will register to vote and will vote based on Your Word and not the words of man. In Jesus Name! Amen

Day 29

Deception of the American People

Matt 24:4 *And Jesus answered and said to them: "Take heed that no one deceives you.*

Eph 5:6 *Let no one deceive you with empty words...*

2 Thessalonians 2:3 *Let no one deceive you by any means...*

Heavenly Father, we come to you in the mighty name of Jesus! You warned us that in the end times many would come to deceive and lead people astray – distracting us from the truth. We are surrounded with fake news. We do not know whom to believe. It is our sincere desire to not be deceived. Holy Spirit, remove the scales from our eyes and sharpen our discernment. We are saturated by the media on all sides that communicates deception, ungodly agendas and political manipulation. We are overwhelmed with information and it is too much for us to bear. Lord, we need Your sovereign touch and guidance to restore integrity and truth to the media, social media, and every form of communication. We know that Satan is the author of lies, confusion and manipulation. We ask for forgiveness for allowing the spirit of lies to dominate over our thinking. We ask for help in this battle to restore truth to our state and nation and clarity of mind to our people.

Lord, there are church leaders that have taken a role in promoting the political agendas that violate Your Word. May heaven forbid! Forgive our state and national leaders for making judgments and passing laws based on current and popular ideologies rather than truth. We need Your word as a plumb line to establish this nation back to righteousness.

The United States of America was founded on the words of the Declaration of Independence: "We hold these truths to be self-evident, that all men are created equal, that they are endowed by their Creator with certain unalienable rights, that among these are <u>life, liberty and the pursuit of happiness.</u>"

Our founders knew that without God we were doomed to deception. So, Father we ask that You forgive us as a nation from foolish lies that oppose Your ways as revealed in Your Word. Help us to be diligent to seek the truth and be careful to express Your amazing love to all. You sent Jesus to rescue us from the penalty of sin by dying on the cross and through Your resurrection, declare the truth that Jesus is Lord of all! Fill our leaders and people with a desire to pursue righteousness, truth, honesty, and justice for our nation. We pray that the American people would be able to see through the deceptions of our age and lay hold of the truths that will unite us as one nation under God!

And now, Lord, I confess that I need help to establish truth in every area of my life. Lord, if I have believed and communicated lies (even in good faith), I ask that You would forgive me and remove the scales from my eyes so that I could discern and perceive more clearly and make righteous judgments that mirror Your word in the way I think, speak, act and vote. Help me cleave to whatever things are true, whatever things are noble, whatever things are just, whatever things are pure, whatever things are lovely, whatever things are of good report, if there is any virtue and if there is anything praiseworthy—meditate on these things. In Jesus mighty name, Amen.

Day 30

The Elections and Voter Fraud

The reality of voter fraud appears as widespread across our country as it is in the American media. Any internet search on this subject yields page after page of instances and accusations. It isn't a new phenomenon in a free democracy, but it seems to be increasing at an alarming rate, fed, in part, by voting practices that require little or no verification of personal ID, by direct manipulation and by the influence of the internet and social media.

There are claims that more votes are cast in the United States than there are actual eligible voters. There are instances of votes being counted from deceased individuals or from those no longer living at the address of record. Requirements for showing identification at polling locations differ from locale to locale. Illegal residents are permitted to get driver's licenses - giving them ID in many states. There is news of ballot harvesting by political operatives, and so on.

Scripture:

Isaiah 5:20 *Woe to those who call evil good, and good evil; Who put darkness for light, and light for darkness; Who put bitter for sweet, and sweet for bitter!*

Proverbs 20:23 *Diverse weights are an abomination to the LORD, And dishonest scales are not good.*

2 Peter 2:19 *While they promise them liberty, they themselves are slaves of corruption; for by whom a person is overcome, by him also he is brought into bondage.*

2 Peter 1:3-4 *as His divine power has given to us all things that pertain to life and godliness, through the knowledge of Him who called us by glory and virtue, ⁴ by which have been given to us exceedingly great and precious promises, that through these you may be partakers of the divine nature, having escaped the corruption that is in the world through lust.*

Deuteronomy 28: 13-14 *...you shall be above only, and not be beneath, if you heed the commandments of the LORD your God, which I command you today, and are careful to observe them. ¹⁴ So you shall not turn aside from any of the words which I command you this day, to the right or the left, ...*

Prayer:

Lord, our hearts are heavy for our nation. We know that we are reaping what we have sown. Corruption is rampant. Lord, we, Your children, confess the sins of our people before You. Father, we confess as sin the motivators of political corruption, and we lay an axe to the greed and quest for corrupt political power within our leaders. Some of this corrupt power grab has fed voter fraud initiatives. Forgive us for the myriad of ways our people have engaged in voter corruption: Ballot rigging, stealing and harvesting, false information in voter guides, un-authorized or dead voters, search engine manipulation, social media censorship, ballot and voting machines being tampered with, and physical or emotional intimidation at the polls.

We confess these ungodly acts as sin as well as every other way Satan has come to kill, steal and destroy our nation's democracy. Our leaders and their helpers have sinned against our people, and against You, Lord. Our legislators and Judges have dealt treacherously with our Constitution, the laws of the land and the American people. By virtue of our American freedoms, we bring our nation before Your throne of grace, asking for forgiveness, mercy and a restoration of righteousness. Renew a right spirit in every person. Our Republic was founded on principles of honesty, uprightness and integrity. We ask that You expose voter fraud hidden in darkness at the highest levels of leadership, at the medium levels of US citizenship and of those who are not US citizens. Bring to justice those who willingly and knowingly participate in and facilitate voter fraud. We pray they would feel conviction, and that the weight of their sin would bring them to confess publicly and repent so that justice can be served, and the sin corrected. Convict those who harvest ballots of moved residents and dead people. Help our county election clerks clean up the rolls of authorized voters. Help them compare signatures and identification with due diligence. Let righteous volunteers come forth! Lord, help our nation deal honestly at the polls. Your Word says You despise unrighteous scales. Voter fraud is an unrighteous weight on the scale. We, Your people and citizens, renounce voter fraud and ask for a sweeping move of honesty and integrity to fall on every American citizen including our leaders! Guide us with wisdom and discernment. Help us flee wickedness and corruption. Protect us from hidden traps or snares of corruption. We lift up our Secretary of State's office and those of every county election clerk's office, and every state engaged in mail-in ballots. We ask for a wave of integrity: one registered voter getting one verified ballot. Let us vote according to righteous scales, Your precepts and no others.

Lord Jesus, as a Christian, I desire to walk in obedience to You, and accurately discern the world of information around me. I, too, have been a victim of corruption. I have listened to and believed lies. I have made unwise choices. Help me make Godly choices and exert my voice with truth according to Your standards. Let every Christian engage in this privilege with wisdom, aptly doing our homework to discern candidates whom You would bless. Help me use godly truthful information to make my decisions. In Jesus Mighty and Righteous Name! Amen!

Day 31

Pray in the Glory – Wrap Up Prayer

To each one who has embraced the call to pray, we encourage you to take your prayer life to the next level as we continue to press deeply into the heart of our Father. It is so important to keep praying biblically and scripturally for our nation, state and city. This is no time to let down our guard. Therefore, we ask you to faithfully continue praying now through the presidential election. It is important that we listen to the Spirit of the Lord, not to our flesh, not to pollsters or poll numbers, not to the media. For we know that tremendous power is released when God's people fervently pray and seek His face. We see in the Bible great examples of the results of prayer: 2 Chronicles 14, 2 Chron. 20, Esther, Acts 16, etc.

Prayer:

We thank You Jesus for Your supreme sacrifice upon the cross and for being seated next to the Father as our Divine mediator, ever interceding on our behalf. We call upon the holy name of our Lord who is ever near, ever present.

We establish every prayer we have just prayed to be acceptable and covered by the blood of Jesus Christ. We seal it up!

Lord, send Your angels to protect the land we just took from the enemy.

We pray that life would inhabit every place that was just uprooted. We pray that all demonic debris would be swept up before the feet of Jesus Christ.

In Jesus' name we come against demonic rulers, authorities, powers, and spiritual forces of evil along with all their roots, works, fruits. Eph 6:12

Lord, we ask for a hedge of protection and cover by the blood of Jesus Christ around every person involved in this warfare. We pray a hedge around our minds, health, families, homes, jobs, finances, possessions, and ministries. Job 1:10, Ps 91

May no harm overtake us, no disaster come near our tent. 'For the Lord will command His angels concerning you to guard you in all your ways'. Shield each intercessor from evil intentions, hide them in the palm of Your hands, and cover them in the cleft of Your rock. For we look to You, our refuge and our fortress, the God in whom we trust! Psalm 91

We declare that we are hidden in You. Psalm 143:9

We release warring angels to go out against the backlash. We quench every fiery dart with our shield of faith. 2 Kings 6:16, Daniel 10:13

We pray for prosperity and increase in every aspect over our lives (wisdom, strength, resourcefulness, divine appointments, protection, joy, fruit of the Spirit, etc.). 3 John 1:2

Oh Lord, I thank You for hearing our cries! Bless all who are faithful warring intercessors! Our hearts are ever reaching heavenward waiting with great anticipation, expecting that something new is about to happen.

Behold, I will do a new thing, Now it shall spring forth; Shall you not know it? I will even make a road in the wilderness and rivers in the desert. Isaiah 43:19

With one voice we cry out "Abba Father, open the flood gates of heaven! Unleash a fresh outpouring of Your blessings to rain down on us. Soak this dry and thirsty land, with a great awakening, a restorative revival. May all who witness Your evident and obvious victorious power stand amazed and bow in humble submission, adoration and obedience. Let Your glory invade the earth displaying the all-powerful dynamic move of You, Lord God Almighty!!"

For the earth will be filled with the knowledge of the glory of the Lord, as the waters cover the sea. Habakkuk 2:14

Come now Lord, and fill our hearts with Your all-consuming fire. Burn up the dross, fan the flame, birth within us a deep and holy passion and a boldness that this world has not seen! Let Your power and Your glory be on display in the church, the bride of Christ! Let her arise from the ash heap with healing in her wings, with her eyes ever gazing upon the author and finisher of her faith, beholding Your power, glory, and Your majesty.

"Holy, holy, holy, Lord God Almighty, Who was and is and is to come!" Rev 4:8

Now, precious prayer warriors, we thank you for praying. We challenge you to get others praying, and pray the 31 Days again! Use this book as a spiritual catapult to pray as the Holy Spirit leads you. We are going to pray as never before until we get breakthrough!

With love to you, from the whole prayer team who wrote this for every intercessor.

Now to the King eternal, immortal, invisible, to God who alone is wise, be honor and glory forever and ever. Amen. 1 Tim 1:17

Healing for the Nation

Federal and State
Executive – Legislative – Judicial Branches

Psalm 139:16-17 *Your eyes saw my substance, being yet unformed. And in Your book they all were written, The days fashioned for me, When as yet there were none of them. How precious also are Your thoughts to me, O God! How great is the sum of them!*

Romans 13:1 *Let every soul be subject to the governing authorities. For there is no authority except from God, and the authorities that exist are appointed by God.*

1 Tim 2:1-4 *Therefore I exhort first of all that supplications, prayers, intercessions,* and *giving of thanks be made for all men, for kings and all who are in authority, that we may lead a quiet and peaceable life in all godliness and reverence. For this* is *good and acceptable in the sight of God our Savior, who desires all men to be saved and to come to the knowledge of the truth.*

Prayer:

Father God, You have written Your Book of Life for us. You have also written it for those in authority over us - our city, state and national leaders in all the branches and departments they serve. We ask that the fear of the Lord be poured out upon them (Prov 9:10). We ask that Your wisdom, love and understanding abide in them so they lead according to Your purposes. Your laws are for our good and for the welfare of our people. Use our leaders to bring forth Your will for our nation. Help us lift the arms of our leaders (Exodus 17:12-13) to encourage them with prayer. We plead Your help and wisdom fill them so that they choose to be godly leaders who honor You in all they do.

We lift up those who are making righteous decrees and voting according to Your precepts. Bless them and give them Your favor. Help them trust in You and articulate Your purposes (Proverbs 3:1-8). Protect them as they go against the flow and give them favor with You and man. May their steps be ordained by You, Lord, so You delight in their ways (Ps 37:23). May goodness and blessing follow them all the days of their lives.

Lord, bind demonic agendas against our leaders and nation. Release Your wisdom, righteousness and strength in Jesus Name! We pray for those who refuse to hear Your voice or honor Your precepts. Lord, have mercy. Turn them to You.

Father, in the name of Jesus, we ask You to forgive the sins of our nation and leaders. You told us to forgive those who have trespassed against us (Matt. 6:9-15). Father, many who serve us have made sinful decisions that violate Your commands thus harming the welfare of our people and nation. In the name of Jesus, we ask You to convict them, to pour out Your Spirit upon them and lead them in confession, repentance and submission to You. Guide them according to Your will and truth to reconcile and correct wrong decisions.

Thank You for hearing our prayers, and for healing our nation and our land according to Your will! May Your will be done and Your Kingdom come, on earth as it is in Heaven! In Jesus Name, Amen.

Editors note: You can find national leaders listed in the pages that follow (Executive Branch, Supreme Court and Legislative Branch).

Genesis of "31 Days of Prayer"

The Fathers Heart Recovery for The Nation

31 Days of Prayer is the most recent prayer book by Tillamook County Wide Prayer Team, inspired by the need for an extreme prayer effort to be lifted up to the Lord by the multitudes throughout the United States in the face of the extraordinary sequence of crises afflicting the United States in 2020.

In 2013, the Tillamook County Wide Prayer Team published its first 40 Days of Prayer in an effort to build unity within the Body of Christ. Since then, we have invited churches in our county and state to join this prayer effort with a new book most years. Every year three-fourths of the churches that span our 75-mile-long county, join together to agree in prayer. We are seeing amazing answers to prayer!

In 2016, the first edition of _50 Days of Prayer_, was published and distributed throughout Tillamook County. It was written by many Christian intercessors. Some are prayer leaders, and some are pastors. We asked our authors from around Oregon to incorporate the scripture into each prayer. What resulted is a powerful tool that leads the reader to pray for topics that impacts them but likely, they never thought to pray for.

In 2019, we felt the Lord was calling us to enlarge the prayer territory. Our 50 Days of Prayer Team began to work with Pray Oregon to build a "Prayer Shield" over Oregon and the Nation. The goal is that on the first of every month more Counties will begin 50 Days of Prayer. This raises a continuous prayer shield over our state and nation all year long! As new communities are added, eventually every state will be bathed in continuous prayer. This prayer can spread like wildfire...

the fire of God to bring healing to our people and nation. If each church catches the fire of His love to lift up passionate prayer over our people and land, we can expect a sweeping move of God.

In 2020, we published a new edition of 50 days of Prayer and customized versions for "Oregon Coast" and for "Central Oregon". These books are available on Amazon. See our website, 50dop.org for more information about these prayer books and for how your group can have a custom version for your area. ~TB

Executive Branch

President **Donald J. Trump**

Vice President **Michael R. Pence**

Secretary of Agriculture **Sonny Perdue**

Attorney General **William Barr**

Director of the Central Intelligence Agency **Gina Haspel**

Secretary of Commerce **Wilbur L. Ross, Jr.**

Secretary of Defense **Mark Esper**

Secretary of Education **Elisabeth Prince DeVos**

Secretary of Energy **Dan Brouillette**

Administrator of the Environmental Protection Agency **Andrew Wheeler**

Secretary of Health and Human Services **Alex Azar**

Acting Secretary of Homeland Security **Chad Wolf**

Secretary of Housing and Urban Development **Benjamin S. Carson, Sr.**

Secretary of the Interior **David Bernhardt**

Secretary of Labor **Eugene Scalia**

Acting Director of the Office of Management and Budget **Russ Vought**

Director of National Intelligence **John Ratcliffe**

Administrator of the Small Business Administration **Jovita Carranza**

Secretary of State **Mike Pompeo**

Secretary of Transportation **Elaine L. Chao**

Secretary of the Treasury **Steven T. Mnuchin**

U.S. Trade Representative **Robert Lighthizer**

Secretary of Veterans Affairs **Robert Wilkie**

White House Chief of Staff **Mark Meadows**

Judicial Branch - Supreme Court

Chief Justice **John G. Roberts**

Associate Justice **Clarence Thomas**

Associate Justice **Ruth Bader Ginsburg**

Associate Justice **Sonia Sotomayor**

Associate Justice **Stephen G. Breyer**

Associate Justice **Samuel A. Alito, Jr.**

Associate Justice **Elena Kagan**

Associate Justice **Neil M Gorsuch**

Associate Justice **Brett Kavanaugh**

Legislative Branch – Senate

State	Senator
Alabama	Richard Shelby
Alabama	Doug Jones
Alaska	Lisa Murkowski
Alaska	Dan Sullivan
Arizona	Kyrsten Sinema
Arizona	Martha McSally
Arkansas	John Boozman
Arkansas	Tom Cotton
California	Dianne Feinstein
California	Kamala Harris
Colorado	Michael Bennet
Colorado	Cory Gardner
Connecti-cut	Richard Blumen-thal
Connecti-cut	Chris Murphy
Delaware	Tom Carper
Delaware	Chris Coons
Florida	Marco Rubio
Florida	Rick Scott
Georgia	David Perdue
Georgia	Kelly Loeffler
Hawaii	Brian Schatz
Hawaii	Mazie Hirono
Idaho	Mike Crapo
Idaho	Jim Risch
Illinois	Dick Durbin
Illinois	Tammy Duckworth
Indiana	Todd Young
Indiana	Mike Braun
Iowa	Chuck Grassley
Iowa	Joni Ernst
Kansas	Pat Roberts
Kansas	Jerry Moran
Kentucky	Mitch McConnell
Kentucky	Rand Paul
Louisiana	Bill Cassidy
Louisiana	John Kennedy
Maine	Susan Collins
Maine	Angus King
Maryland	Ben Cardin
Maryland	Chris Van Hollen
Massachu-setts	Elizabeth Warren

Massachusetts	Ed Markey	**New York**	Chuck Schumer
		New York	Kirsten Gillibrand
Michigan	Debbie Stabenow		
Michigan	Gary Peters	**North Carolina**	Richard Burr
		North Carolina	Thom Tillis
Minnesota	Amy Klobuchar		
Minnesota	Tina Smith	**North Dakota**	John Hoeven
Mississippi	Roger Wicker	North Dakota	Kevin Cramer
Mississippi	Cindy Hyde-Smith		
		Ohio	Sherrod Brown
Missouri	Roy Blunt	Ohio	Rob Portman
Missouri	Josh Hawley		
		Oklahoma	Jim Inhofe
Montana	Jon Tester	Oklahoma	James Lankford
Montana	Steve Daines		
		Oregon	Ron Wyden
Nebraska	Deb Fischer	Oregon	Jeff Merkley
Nebraska	Ben Sasse		
		Pennsylvania	Bob Casey Jr.
Nevada	Catherine Cortez Masto	Pennsylvania	Pat Toomey
Nevada	Jacky Rosen		
		Rhode Island	Jack Reed
New Hampshire	Jeanne Shaheen	Rhode Island	Sheldon Whitehouse
New Hampshire	Maggie Hassan		
		South Carolina	Lindsey Graham
New Jersey	Bob Menendez	South Carolina	Tim Scott
New Jersey	Cory Booker		
		South Dakota	John Thune
New Mexico	Tom Udall	South Dakota	Mike Rounds
New Mexico	Martin Heinrich		

Tennessee	Lamar Alexander		
Tennessee	Marsha Blackburn	**Washington**	Patty Murray
		Washington	Maria Cantwell
Texas	John Cornyn		
Texas	Ted Cruz	**West Virginia**	Joe Manchin
		West Virginia	Shelley Moore Capito
Utah	Mike Lee		
Utah	Mitt Romney	**Wisconsin**	Ron Johnson
		Wisconsin	Tammy Baldwin
Vermont	Patrick Leahy		
Vermont	Bernie Sanders	**Wyoming**	Mike Enzi
		Wyoming	John Barrasso
Virginia	Mark Warner		
Virginia	Tim Kaine		

Legislative Branch
House of Representatives

Alabama

District	Name
1st	Byrne, Bradley
2nd	Roby, Martha
3rd	Rogers, Mike
4th	Aderholt, Robert
5th	Brooks, Mo
6th	Palmer, Gary
7th	Sewell, Terri A.

Alaska

District	Name
At Large	Young, Don

American Samoa

District	Name
Delegate	Radewagen, Amata

Arizona

District	Name
1st	O'Halleran, Tom
2nd	Kirkpatrick, Ann
3rd	Grijalva, Raul
4th	Gosar, Paul A.
5th	Biggs, Andy
6th	Schweikert, David
7th	Gallego, Ruben

| 8th | Lesko, Debbie |
| 9th | Stanton, Greg |

Arkansas

District	Name
1st	Crawford, Rick
2nd	Hill, French
3rd	Womack, Steve
4th	Westerman, Bruce

California

District	Name
1st	LaMalfa, Doug
2nd	Huffman, Jared
3rd	Garamendi, John
4th	McClintock, Tom
5th	Thompson, Mike
6th	Matsui, Doris O.
7th	Bera, Ami
8th	Cook, Paul
9th	McNerney, Jerry
10th	Harder, Josh
11th	DeSaulnier, Mark
12th	Pelosi, Nancy
13th	Lee, Barbara
14th	Speier, Jackie

15th	Swalwell, Eric
16th	Costa, Jim
17th	Khanna, Ro
18th	Eshoo, Anna G.
19th	Lofgren, Zoe
20th	Panetta, Jimmy
21st	Cox, TJ
22nd	Nunes, Devin
23rd	McCarthy, Kevin
24th	Carbajal, Salud
25th	Garcia, Mike
26th	Brownley, Julia
27th	Chu, Judy
28th	Schiff, Adam
29th	Cárdenas, Tony
30th	Sherman, Brad
31st	Aguilar, Pete
32nd	Napolitano, Grace
33rd	Lieu, Ted
34th	Gomez, Jimmy
35th	Torres, Norma
36th	Ruiz, Raul
37th	Bass, Karen
38th	Sánchez, Linda
39th	Cisneros, Gilbert Ray Jr.
40th	Roybal-Allard, Lucille
41st	Takano, Mark
42nd	Calvert, Ken
43rd	Waters, Maxine
44th	Barragán, Nanette
45th	Porter, Katie
46th	Correa, J. Luis
47th	Lowenthal, Alan
48th	Rouda, Harley
49th	Levin, Mike
50th	Hunter, Duncan - Vacancy
51st	Vargas, Juan
52nd	Peters, Scott
53rd	Davis, Susan

Colorado

District	Name
1st	DeGette, Diana
2nd	Neguse, Joe
3rd	Tipton, Scott
4th	Buck, Ken
5th	Lamborn, Doug
6th	Crow, Jason
7th	Perlmutter, Ed

Connecticut

District	Name
1st	Larson, John B.
2nd	Courtney, Joe
3rd	DeLauro, Rosa L.
4th	Himes, Jim
5th	Hayes, Jahana

Delaware

District	Name
At Large	Blunt Rochester, Lisa

97

District of Columbia

District	Name
Delegate	Norton, Eleanor Holmes

Florida

District	Name
1st	Gaetz, Matt
2nd	Dunn, Neal
3rd	Yoho, Ted
4th	Rutherford, John
5th	Lawson, Al
6th	Waltz, Michael
7th	Murphy, Stephanie
8th	Posey, Bill
9th	Soto, Darren
10th	Demings, Val
11th	Webster, Daniel
12th	Bilirakis, Gus M.
13th	Crist, Charlie
14th	Castor, Kathy
15th	Spano, Ross
16th	Buchanan, Vern
17th	Steube, W. Gregory
18th	Mast, Brian
19th	Rooney, Francis
20th	Hastings, Alcee L.
21st	Frankel, Lois
22nd	Deutch, Ted
23rd	Wasserman Schultz, Debbie
24th	Wilson, Frederica
25th	Diaz-Balart, Mario
26th	Mucarsel-Powell, Debbie
27th	Shalala, Donna E.

Georgia

District	Name
1st	Carter, Buddy
2nd	Bishop Jr., Sanford D.
3rd	Ferguson, A. Drew
4th	Johnson, Henry C. "Hank" Jr.
5th	Lewis, John
6th	McBath, Lucy
7th	Woodall, Robert
8th	Scott, Austin
9th	Collins, Doug
10th	Hice, Jody
11th	Loudermilk, Barry
12th	Allen, Rick
13th	Scott, David
14th	Graves, Tom

Guam

District	Name
Delegate	San Nicolas, Michael F. Q.

Hawaii

District	Name
1st	Case, Ed
2nd	Gabbard, Tulsi

Idaho

District	Name
1st	Fulcher, Russ
2nd	Simpson, Mike

Illinois

District	Name
1st	Rush, Bobby L.
2nd	Kelly, Robin
3rd	Lipinski, Daniel
4th	García, Jesús "Chuy"
5th	Quigley, Mike
6th	Casten, Sean
7th	Davis, Danny K.
8th	Krishna-moorthi, Raja
9th	Schakowsky, Jan
10th	Schneider, Bradley
11th	Foster, Bill
12th	Bost, Mike
13th	Davis, Rodney
14th	Underwood, Lauren
15th	Shimkus, John
16th	Kinzinger, Adam
17th	Bustos, Cheri
18th	LaHood, Darin

Indiana

District	Name
1st	Visclosky, Peter
2nd	Walorski, Jackie
3rd	Banks, Jim
4th	Baird, James
5th	Brooks, Susan W.
6th	Pence, Greg
7th	Carson, André
8th	Bucshon, Larry
9th	Hollingsworth, Trey

Iowa

District	Name
1st	Finkenauer, Abby
2nd	Loebsack, David
3rd	Axne, Cynthia
4th	King, Steve

Kansas

District	Name
1st	Marshall, Roger
2nd	Watkins, Steve
3rd	Davids, Sharice
4th	Estes, Ron

Kentucky

District	Name
1st	Comer, James
2nd	Guthrie, S. Brett
3rd	Yarmuth, John A.

District	Name
4th	Massie, Thomas
5th	Rogers, Harold
6th	Barr, Andy

Louisiana

District	Name
1st	Scalise, Steve
2nd	Richmond, Cedric
3rd	Higgins, Clay
4th	Johnson, Mike
5th	Abraham, Ralph
6th	Graves, Garret

Maine

District	Name
1st	Pingree, Chellie
2nd	Golden, Jared

Maryland

District	Name
1st	Harris, Andy
2nd	Ruppersberger, C. A. Dutch
3rd	Sarbanes, John P.
4th	Brown, Anthony
5th	Hoyer, Steny H.
6th	Trone, David
7th	Mfume, Kweisi
8th	Raskin, Jamie

Massachusetts

District	Name
1st	Neal, Richard E.
2nd	McGovern, James
3rd	Trahan, Lori
4th	Kennedy III, Joseph P.
5th	Clark, Katherine
6th	Moulton, Seth
7th	Pressley, Ayanna
8th	Lynch, Stephen F.
9th	Keating, William

Michigan

District	Name
1st	Bergman, Jack
2nd	Huizenga, Bill
3rd	Amash, Justin
4th	Moolenaar, John
5th	Kildee, Daniel
6th	Upton, Fred
7th	Walberg, Tim
8th	Slotkin, Elissa
9th	Levin, Andy
10th	Mitchell, Paul
11th	Stevens, Haley
12th	Dingell, Debbie
13th	Tlaib, Rashida
14th	Lawrence, Brenda

Minnesota

District	Name
1st	Hagedorn, Jim

District	Name
2nd	Craig, Angie
3rd	Phillips, Dean
4th	McCollum, Betty
5th	Omar, Ilhan
6th	Emmer, Tom
7th	Peterson, Collin C.
8th	Stauber, Pete

Mississippi

District	Name
1st	Kelly, Trent
2nd	Thompson, Bennie G.
3rd	Guest, Michael
4th	Palazzo, Steven

Missouri

District	Name
1st	Clay Jr., William "Lacy"
2nd	Wagner, Ann
3rd	Luetkemeyer, Blaine
4th	Hartzler, Vicky
5th	Cleaver, Emanuel
6th	Graves, Sam
7th	Long, Billy
8th	Smith, Jason

Montana

District	Name
At Large	Gianforte, Greg

Nebraska

District	Name
1st	Fortenberry, Jeff
2nd	Bacon, Don
3rd	Smith, Adrian

Nevada

District	Name
1st	Titus, Dina
2nd	Amodei, Mark
3rd	Lee, Susie
4th	Horsford, Steven

New Hampshire

District	Name
1st	Pappas, Chris
2nd	Kuster, Ann

New Jersey

District	Name
1st	Norcross, Donald
2nd	Van Drew, Jefferson
3rd	Kim, Andy
4th	Smith, Chris
5th	Gottheimer, Josh
6th	Pallone Jr., Frank
7th	Malinowski, Tom
8th	Sires, Albio
9th	Pascrell Jr., Bill
10th	Payne Jr., Donald

District	Name
11th	Sherrill, Mikie
12th	Watson Coleman, Bonnie

New Mexico

District	Name
1st	Haaland, Debra
2nd	Torres Small, Xochitl
3rd	Luján, Ben R.

New York

District	Name
1st	Zeldin, Lee
2nd	King, Pete
3rd	Suozzi, Thomas
4th	Rice, Kathleen
5th	Meeks, Gregory W.
6th	Meng, Grace
7th	Velázquez, Nydia M.
8th	Jeffries, Hakeem
9th	Clarke, Yvette D.
10th	Nadler, Jerrold
11th	Rose, Max
12th	Maloney, Carolyn
13th	Espaillat, Adriano
14th	Ocasio-Cortez, Alexandria
15th	Serrano, José E.
16th	Engel, Eliot
17th	Lowey, Nita
18th	Maloney, Sean Patrick
19th	Delgado, Antonio
20th	Tonko, Paul D.
21st	Stefanik, Elise
22nd	Brindisi, Anthony
23rd	Reed, Tom
24th	Katko, John
25th	Morelle, Joseph
26th	Higgins, Brian
27th	Collins, Chris - Vacancy

North Carolina

District	Name
1st	Butterfield, G.K.
2nd	Holding, George
3rd	Murphy, Gregory Francis
4th	Price, David
5th	Foxx, Virginia
6th	Walker, Mark
7th	Rouzer, David
8th	Hudson, Richard
9th	Bishop, Dan
10th	McHenry, Patrick T.
11th	Meadows, Mark - Vacancy
12th	Adams, Alma

13th	Budd, Ted

North Dakota

District	Name
At Large	Armstrong, Kelly

Northern Mariana Is

District	Name
Delegate	Sablan, Gregorio

Ohio

District	Name
1st	Chabot, Steve
2nd	Wenstrup, Brad
3rd	Beatty, Joyce
4th	Jordan, Jim
5th	Latta, Robert E.
6th	Johnson, Bill
7th	Gibbs, Bob
8th	Davidson, Warren
9th	Kaptur, Marcy
10th	Turner, Michael
11th	Fudge, Marcia L.
12th	Balderson, Troy
13th	Ryan, Tim
14th	Joyce, David
15th	Stivers, Steve
16th	Gonzalez, Anthony

Oklahoma

District	Name
1st	Hern, Kevin
2nd	Mullin, Markwayne
3rd	Lucas, Frank
4th	Cole, Tom
5th	Horn, Kendra

Oregon

District	Name
1st	Bonamici, Suzanne
2nd	Walden, Greg
3rd	Blumenauer, Earl
4th	DeFazio, Peter
5th	Schrader, Kurt

Pennsylvania

District	Name
1st	Fitzpatrick, Brian
2nd	Boyle, Brendan
3rd	Evans, Dwight
4th	Dean, Madeleine
5th	Scanlon, Mary Gay
6th	Houlahan, Chrissy
7th	Wild, Susan
8th	Cartwright, Matt
9th	Meuser, Daniel
10th	Perry, Scott
11th	Smucker, Lloyd
12th	Keller, Fred
13th	Joyce, John

14th	Reschenthaler, Guy
15th	Thompson, Glenn
16th	Kelly, Mike
17th	Lamb, Conor
18th	Doyle, Michael

Puerto Rico

District	Name
Resident Commissioner	González-Colón, Jenniffer

Rhode Island

District	Name
1st	Cicilline, David
2nd	Langevin, Jim

South Carolina

District	Name
1st	Cunningham, Joe
2nd	Wilson, Joe
3rd	Duncan, Jeff
4th	Timmons, William
5th	Norman, Ralph
6th	Clyburn, James E.
7th	Rice, Tom

South Dakota

District	Name
At Large	Johnson, Dusty

Tennessee

District	Name
1st	Roe, Phil
2nd	Burchett, Tim
3rd	Fleischmann, Chuck
4th	DesJarlais, Scott
5th	Cooper, Jim
6th	Rose, John W.
7th	Green, Mark
8th	Kustoff, David
9th	Cohen, Steve

Texas

District	Name
1st	Gohmert, Louie
2nd	Crenshaw, Dan
3rd	Taylor, Van
4th	Ratcliffe, John - Vacancy
5th	Gooden, Lance
6th	Wright, Ron
7th	Fletcher, Lizzie
8th	Brady, Kevin
9th	Green, Al
10th	McCaul, Michael T.
11th	Conaway, K. Michael
12th	Granger, Kay
13th	Thornberry, Mac
14th	Weber, Randy
15th	Gonzalez, Vicente
16th	Escobar, Veronica

17th	Flores, Bill
18th	Jackson Lee, Sheila
19th	Arrington, Jodey
20th	Castro, Joaquin
21st	Roy, Chip
22nd	Olson, Pete
23rd	Hurd, Will
24th	Marchant, Kenny
25th	Williams, Roger
26th	Burgess, Michael
27th	Cloud, Michael
28th	Cuellar, Henry
29th	Garcia, Sylvia
30th	Johnson, Eddie Bernice
31st	Carter, John
32nd	Allred, Colin
33rd	Veasey, Marc
34th	Vela, Filemon
35th	Doggett, Lloyd
36th	Babin, Brian

Utah

District	Name
1st	Bishop, Rob
2nd	Stewart, Chris
3rd	Curtis, John R.
4th	McAdams, Ben

Vermont

District	Name

At Large	Welch, Peter

Virgin Islands

District	Name
Delegate	Plaskett, Stacey

Virginia

District	Name
1st	Wittman, Robert J.
2nd	Luria, Elaine
3rd	Scott, Robert C.
4th	McEachin, A. Donald
5th	Riggleman, Denver
6th	Cline, Ben
7th	Spanberger, Abigail
8th	Beyer, Don
9th	Griffith, Morgan
10th	Wexton, Jennifer
11th	Connolly, Gerald E. "Gerry"

Washington

District	Name
1st	DelBene, Suzan
2nd	Larsen, Rick
3rd	Herrera Beutler, Jaime
4th	Newhouse, Dan
5th	Rodgers, Cathy McMorris

District	Name
6th	Kilmer, Derek
7th	Jayapal, Pramila
8th	Schrier, Kim
9th	Smith, Adam
10th	Heck, Denny

West Virginia

District	Name
1st	McKinley, David
2nd	Mooney, Alex
3rd	Miller, Carol

Wisconsin

District	Name
1st	Steil, Bryan
2nd	Pocan, Mark
3rd	Kind, Ron
4th	Moore, Gwen
5th	Sensenbrenner, F. James
6th	Grothman, Glenn
7th	Tiffany, Thomas P.
8th	Gallagher, Mike

Wyoming

District	Name
At Large	Cheney, Liz

Made in the USA
Middletown, DE
19 August 2020

15776530R00066